YAS

The Kennedy Assassination

The Kennedy Assassination

New and future titles in the series include:

- Alien Abductions
- Angels
- The Bermuda Triangle
- The Curse of King Tut
- Dragons
- ESP
- Extinction of the Dinosaurs
- Haunted Houses
- King Arthur
- The Loch Ness Monster
- Pyramids
- Stonehenge
- UFOs
- Unicorns
- Vampires
- Witches

The Mystery Library

The Kennedy Assassination

Stuart A. Kallen

LUCENT
BOOKS®

THOMSON
———★———™
GALE

San Diego • Detroit • New York • San Francisco • Cleveland • New Haven, Conn. • Waterville, Maine • London • Munich

On Cover: President and Mrs. John F. Kennedy ride in the
fateful Dallas motorcade, November 22, 1963.

LIBRARY OF CONGRESS CATALOGING-IN-PUBLICATION DATA

Kallen, Stuart A., 1955–
    The Kennedy assassination / by Stuart A. Kallen.
        v. cm. — (The mystery library)
Includes bibliographical references (p.) and index.
Contents: Who killed JFK — Death in Dallas — How many bullets were fired? — Who
was Oswald and did he kill the president? — Did the Mafia kill Kennedy? — Was the
government involved?
        ISBN 1-59018-128-X (hardback : alk. paper)
    1. Kennedy, John F. (John Fitzgerald), 1917–1963 — Assassination — Juvenile
literature. [1. Kennedy, John F. (John Fitzgerald), 1917–1963 — Assassination.]
I. Title. II. Series: Mystery library (Lucent Books)
E842.9.K26 2003
364.15'24'097309046—dc21
                                                                    2002156115

Contents

Foreword

In Shakespeare's immortal play, *Hamlet*, the young Danish aristocrat Horatio has clearly been astonished and disconcerted by his encounter with a ghost-like apparition on the castle battlements. "There are more things in heaven and earth," his friend Hamlet assures him, "than are dreamt of in your philosophy."

Many people today would readily agree with Hamlet that the world and the vast universe surrounding it are teeming with wonders and oddities that remain largely outside the realm of present human knowledge or understanding. How did the universe begin? What caused the dinosaurs to become extinct? Was the lost continent of Atlantis a real place or merely legendary? Does a monstrous creature lurk beneath the surface of Scotland's Loch Ness? These are only a few of the intriguing questions that remain unanswered, despite the many great strides made by science in recent centuries.

Lucent Books' Mystery Library series is dedicated to exploring these and other perplexing, sometimes bizarre, and often disturbing or frightening wonders. Each volume in the series presents the best-known tales, incidents, and evidence surrounding the topic in question. Also included are the opinions and theories of scientists and other experts who have attempted to unravel and solve the ongoing mystery. And supplementing this information is a fulsome list of sources for further reading, providing the reader with the means to pursue the topic further.

The Mystery Library will satisfy every young reader's fascination for the unexplained. As one of history's greatest scientists, physicist Albert Einstein, put it:

> The most beautiful thing we can experience is the mysterious. It is the source of all true art and science. He to whom this emotion is a stranger, who can no longer wonder and stand rapt in awe, is as good as dead: his eyes are closed.

Who Killed JFK?

The early 1960s were a time of optimism and prosperity in the United States. Although the country faced many problems both at home and abroad, a majority of Americans believed that President John F. Kennedy (JFK) was leading the country in the right direction.

When forty-three-year-old Kennedy was elected president in 1960 he was the youngest man to ever move into the White House. With his charming wife Jacqueline and two small children, the Kennedys projected an image of warmth and fun. They were widely admired by millions of Americans as the ideal family. This admiration was also reflected in polling numbers that showed Kennedy enjoying an 83 percent approval rating in 1961.

Kennedy had an idealistic vision for the United States. He saw America in the 1960s as a "New Frontier" in which unknown perils but also great potential lay ahead. In keeping with this vision of America, Kennedy established the Peace Corps to encourage young people to perform social and humanitarian service overseas, helping people in Third World countries in matters of health, agriculture, and education. Kennedy also initiated the space program, promising that the United States would land a man on the moon within a decade.

All the President's Enemies

Even as the president presented an ambitious agenda, there were many negative forces working against his policies in the United States and abroad. Throughout the South, white police officers often beat and arrested African Americans as they demonstrated peacefully to end segregation. Kennedy supported civil rights, hired African Americans in his administration, and appointed black judges, such as Thurgood Marshall, to federal courts. This created extreme

Many Americans believed that President John F. Kennedy, wife Jacqueline, and children John and Caroline represented the ideal family.

resentment and hostility toward the president from many white southerners, and the president received numerous death threats from racists who violently disagreed with his policies. The president's civil rights policies were also hurting him politically; by October 1963 Kennedy's approval rating had slipped to 59 percent and *Newsweek* magazine reported that the civil rights issue had cost Kennedy 3.5 million white votes, adding that no Democrat in the White House had ever been so disliked in the South.

Kennedy was also troubled by the activities of organized crime. The Mafia, in particular, was at the height of its power in the early sixties. Illegal drug sales, gambling, and prostitution were among the Mafia's most profitable ventures. It controlled multibillion dollar operations in dozens of cities across America.

In December 1961 the president's brother, Attorney General Robert Kennedy, ordered the Federal Bureau of Investigation (FBI) to arrest and jail high-ranking Mafia leaders. The president supported this move by drafting new crime laws that strengthened the FBI's jurisdiction over organized crime cases. With federal agents threatening their crime empires, powerful Mafia bosses such as Sam Giancana, Carlos Marcello, and Santos Trafficante swore vengeance on the Kennedy brothers.

Even as the FBI was trying to jail Giancana and Trafficante, these same Mafia bosses were secretly working with the Central Intelligence Agency (CIA) to eliminate Communist Cuban dictator Fidel Castro. The Mafia had long controlled dozens of casinos in Cuba, a small island nation ninety miles off the coast of Florida. But in 1959 Castro led a successful Communist revolution and evicted the Mafia.

Together, the CIA and members of the Mafia participated in a series of failed plots to kill Castro. When Kennedy discovered the CIA was working with the Mafia, he was horrified and ordered the Agency to stop these activities. When he later found out that his orders had been ignored

Cuban leader Fidel Castro was the target of several failed assassination attempts organized by the CIA and members of the Mafia.

and the plots were continuing, Kennedy sent the FBI and local law enforcement agencies to shut down the Agency's secret training camps on southern Florida's No Name Key and on Lake Pontchartrain in New Orleans. Kennedy then fired long-time CIA director Allen Dulles along with many of his top agents. Vowing to dismantle the powerful spy agency, Kennedy said he would "splinter the CIA into a thousand pieces and scatter it into the winds."[1]

The Bay of Pigs Fiasco

Cuba caused the president other problems as well. Kennedy's predecessor Dwight D. Eisenhower had ordered the CIA to train Cuban exiles to invade the island and overthrow Castro. The anti-Castro forces were to land in an area called the Bay of Pigs. Assured by the CIA that native Cubans would welcome the liberating forces—and that the role of the Americans would remain secret— Kennedy approved the invasion. In April 1961, about fifteen hundred Cuban exiles invaded Cuba. At the last minute, however, Kennedy called off U.S. air support fearing that if America's role in the invasion was exposed, it would earn worldwide condemnation. Without the air support the anti-Castro Cubans were quickly defeated. About one hundred were killed and the rest taken prisoner. After the Bay of Pigs fiasco became public, Kennedy was harshly criticized by the fervently anti-Castro Cuban exiles and other anti-Communist groups as well as CIA agents.

By angering the anti-Castro Cubans, the Mafia, rogue forces within the CIA and FBI, and southern racists, Kennedy made some powerful enemies during his few short years in office. When he was assassinated in November 1963, some people wondered if members of one or more of these groups had been involved in the president's murder. These people doubted the official government version of events that blamed a lone gunman named Lee Harvey Oswald. When Oswald was shot to death two days after Kennedy's murder by a nightclub owner named Jack Ruby, one of the longest-running controversies in American history began—and it remains under discussion four decades after the actual event. While thousands of important facts relating to the case have been uncovered during the years following the president's death, the mystery remains: Who killed President John F. Kennedy, and why?

Chapter 1

Death in Dallas

The morning of November 22, 1963, dawned cool and rainy in Dallas, Texas. By the time President John F. Kennedy and his wife Jacqueline arrived on *Air Force One* at 11:35 A.M., however, it was seventy degrees and sunny. Kennedy had traveled to Dallas to strengthen his political support for his second run for president in November 1964, and Texas would play an important role in his re-election. Kennedy's vice president, Lyndon Baines Johnson, was a popular Texan, but the state's large number of electoral votes had gone to the president's opponent, Republican Richard Nixon, in 1960. Kennedy wanted to win Texas in 1964, despite the presence of a powerful right-wing contingent that strongly disliked the charismatic Democratic president and his policies. These political opponents accused Kennedy of being soft on the Communist governments of Cuba, Vietnam, and the Soviet Union.

Upon landing at Dallas's Love Field, the president and First Lady were met by Texas governor John Connally and his wife. The two couples climbed into the blue 1961 Lincoln four-door convertible for a short drive to a luncheon at the Dallas Trade Mart convention center where Kennedy would give a speech to twenty-five hundred local business and civic leaders. The president and the First Lady sat in the back seat of the official presidential limousine while Connally and his wife Nellie sat on fold-down jump seats in front of the Kennedys. Secret Service Agent William Greer was at the wheel.

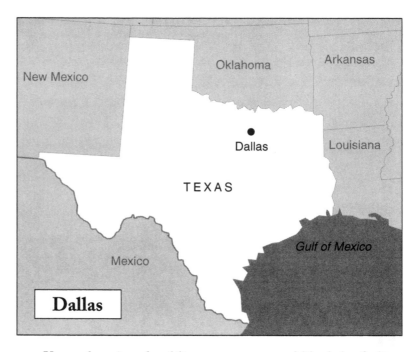

Dallas

Kennedy enjoyed public appearances and liked the feeling of closeness he got from strolling or riding through crowds, waving and shaking hands. He told his aides that he liked to "see and be seen."[2] He made it known that he strongly disliked the clear plastic "bubbletop" that fit over the presidential limousine; he felt this barrier enforced a separation from the crowds. The bubbletop was not bulletproof but it did provide some protection for the president. Despite safety concerns expressed by Secret Service agents, the bubbletop was removed so that the president could ride through the streets of Dallas in an open limousine.

Although the president was extremely popular across the United States, Dallas was not a friendly town to politicians such as Kennedy who supported racial integration, a nuclear test ban treaty with the Soviet Union, and diplomatic appeasement of Communist governments. In fact Dallas had recently been dubbed the "City of Hate" by the press because of several incidents. Only a month before Kennedy arrived, U.S. ambassador to the United Nations Adlai Stevenson was cursed, spat upon, and heckled by Republican protesters, one of whom hit him over the head with a protest sign.

On the day Kennedy arrived, the *Dallas Morning News* ran a full-page ad placed by three Dallas businessmen that shrilly criticized the president's policies and accused him of being "soft on Communists . . . and ultra-leftists in America."[3] And even before the motorcade began, handbills were circulated throughout the crowd that showed a profile and front view of President Kennedy, similar to a police mug shot, with a caption that reads "Wanted for Treason: This Man Is Wanted for Treasonous Activities Against the United States."[4]

President and Mrs. Kennedy are delighted with their warm reception in Dallas. The president insisted that the protective bubbletop be removed from their limousine.

Murder in Dealey Plaza

Such was the political atmosphere when Kennedy's limousine rolled out of Love Field and headed through downtown Dallas on Main Street. Although it was not the most direct route to the Trade Mart, the presidential motorcade turned right from Main onto Houston Street, drove one block, then made a sharp left onto Elm Street. As the limousine crawled passed the seven-story Texas School Book Depository, a brick warehouse where schoolbooks were stored, the president and First Lady smiled and waved at the crowds. Mrs. Connally turned to the president and said, "Mr. President, you can't say that Dallas doesn't love you." The president replied "That's obvious."[5]

Once past the School Book Depository the motorcade approached a small grassy area called Dealey Plaza, named after George Bannerman Dealey, former publisher of the *Dallas Morning News*. The plaza was a small park bounded on the north by Elm Street, on the south by Commerce Street, and on the west by a railroad bridge known as the triple underpass because Main, Commerce, and Elm passed under it.

In order to make the 120 degree turn from Main onto Elm the presidential motorcade was forced to crawl along at eleven miles per hour. This operation violated Secret Service regulations stating that, for the president's safety, a motorcade should always maintain speeds of twenty miles per hour or more.

To the president's right, a small hill, now known as the "grassy knoll," rose up from the roadway with a passageway of columns called a colonnade at the top of the hill. A picket fence extended from the colonnade, separating Dealey Plaza from a busy railroad yard and a dirt parking lot used by the Sheriff's Department.

Twelve seconds after a large clock on a billboard atop the Texas School Book Depository changed to 12:30 P.M., the sound of gunfire filled the air in Dealey Plaza. In his

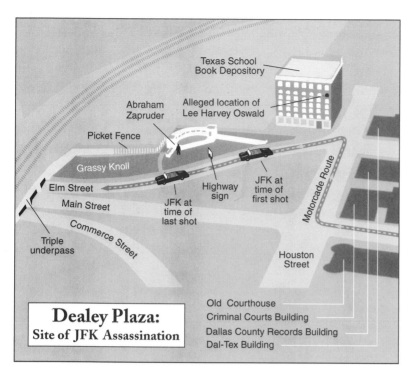

Texas School
Book Depository

Abraham
Zapruder

Alleged location of
Lee Harvey Oswald

Picket Fence

Grassy Knoll

Elm Street

Main Street

Highway
sign

JFK at
time of
first shot

Motorcade Route

JFK at
time of
last shot

Commerce Street

Triple
underpass

Houston
Street

Dealey Plaza:
Site of JFK Assassination

Old Courthouse
Criminal Courts Building
Dallas County Records Building
Dal-Tex Building

book *Conspiracy*, Anthony Summers describes the sequence
of events that followed:

> According to a Secret Serviceman in the car, the
> President said, "My God, I'm hit." He lurched in his
> seat, both hands clawing toward his throat. Directly
> in front of the President, Governor Connally heard
> one shot and was then hit himself. He screamed. . . .
> Then came more gunfire. The President fell violently
> backwards and to his left, his head exploding in a
> halo of brain tissue, blood and bone. To Mrs.
> Connally it "was like buckshot falling all over us." As
> the car finally gathered speed, Mrs. Kennedy believed
> she cried, "I love you, Jack." From the front seat the
> Governor's wife heard her exclaim, "Jack . . . they've
> killed my husband." Then, "I have his brains in my
> hand." This last [sentence] Mrs. Kennedy repeated
> time and time again. It was over.[6]

During the shooting, Governor Connally sustained wounds in his back, right chest, right wrist, and left thigh. As the bullets rained down, Agent Clint Hill, who had been running behind the car, jumped on the bumper of the limousine and crawled up on the trunk to block the president and Mrs. Kennedy from further shots.

The barrage of shots lasted little more than five seconds. After the sound of gunfire stopped echoing through Dealey Plaza, Greer accelerated, driving to Parkland Memorial Hospital where doctors worked in vain to save the president's life. Their efforts failed and Kennedy was pronounced dead at 1:00 P.M. Although Connally was badly wounded, he survived.

Oswald's Curtain Rods

Through purchase records, police were able to trace the Mannlicher-Carcano rifle found in the Texas School Book Depository to Lee Harvey Oswald. The suspect in the president's murder had purchased the rifle for fourteen dollars from a mail order catalog using the alias Alek J. Hidell. In *Conspiracy* Anthony Summers explains how Oswald allegedly smuggled the gun into the School Book Depository on the day of Kennedy's murder:

On the eve of the assassination Oswald had asked a fellow employee, Buell Frazier, to drive him to [the rooming house where his estranged wife Marina Oswald lived]. Frazier quoted him as saying, "I'm going home to get some curtain rods . . . to put in an apartment." Oswald had then stayed the night with his wife and left the next morning before she was up, at 7:15 A.M. He then

walked over to Frazier's house, just a few doors away, to get a lift into work. Frazier's sister noticed that Oswald was now carrying a heavy brown bag, and Frazier asked about it as the two men drove into the city. Oswald said something about "curtain rods," and Frazier remembered he had mentioned rods the night before. At the Texas School Book Depository, Oswald walked ahead into the building, holding the package tucked under his right armpit.

After the assassination, during their search of the sixth floor, police found a brown paper bag large enough to have contained the Mannlicher-Carcano rifle. It appeared to be home-made. The FBI later found a palm print and a fingerprint on the bag, and these matched Oswald's right palm and his left index finger.

The Aftermath

Immediately after the limousine sped off, chaos reigned in Dealey Plaza. Dozens of people had dived to the ground during the shooting, and police were running everywhere. About two hundred onlookers and police spontaneously ran up the grassy knoll to the parking lot behind the colonnade, convinced that the shots came from that area. They were turned back by men that witnesses determined were Secret Service agents because of the badges they displayed.

Meanwhile, Officer Marion Baker pulled out his revolver and ran into the School Book Depository after seeing startled pigeons fly off from the roof as gunshots rang out. About ninety seconds after the shooting, Baker, accompanied by building supervisor Roy Truly, met up with Lee Harvey Oswald in the second-floor lunchroom. After Oswald was identified by Truly as an employee of the School Book Depository, Baker moved on to search the rest of the building. Several minutes later, a seemingly nonchalant Oswald walked out of the School Book Depository and boarded a city bus.

About twenty minutes after the shooting, three deputy sheriffs searching the building found three spent bullet cartridges in an area now known as the "sniper's nest" in the southwest corner of the sixth floor. These shell casings lay near a half-opened window that overlooked Elm Street and the motorcade route. Moments later, police searching the northeast corner of the sixth floor found a World War II vintage, Italian-made Mannlicher-Carcano rifle with a telescopic sight. It had been stashed between two pallets piled with cartons of books.

Picking Up Oswald

While police officials scrambled to identify an assassin, Oswald's bus got caught in heavy traffic. Oswald left the bus and found a taxicab to take him to the boardinghouse where he was living at that time.

About thirty minutes after the assassination, Oswald entered the boardinghouse, changed his shirt, and grabbed a Smith and Wesson .38-caliber revolver from his bureau. Police say Oswald then left his house at 1:04 P.M. and had walked about eight-tenths of a mile from his home when a Dallas police officer named J.D. Tippit apparently stopped him for questioning around 1:12 P.M. Tippit was shot dead and when reports of the shooting were broadcast over the police radio, squad cars quickly converged on the nearby Texas Theater where a witness claimed to have seen Oswald acting suspiciously before sneaking into the movie house without paying.

Police officers found Oswald sitting in a seat in the nearly empty theater. When Officer Nick McDonald approached him, Oswald punched the officer in the face. According to McDonald, a struggle ensued during which time Oswald pulled out his pistol. During the scuffle, Oswald tried to fire his gun at the officers but it jammed. Oswald was finally punched in the face and overpowered by the police, causing him to yell out "I am not resisting arrest! Police brutality!"[7] The officers then arrested Oswald and transported him to Dallas police headquarters. During the ride to the station, officers claimed the suspect was calm and collected, no more ruffled than if he was simply being arrested for sneaking into the movie theater.

Meanwhile, at 2:38 P.M., a little more than three hours after the Kennedys had landed in Dallas, vice president Lyndon Johnson was sworn in as president of the United States. A photograph of that moment shows Johnson standing in the aisle of *Air Force One* taking the vow with his right hand raised, flanked by a dazed Jacqueline Kennedy, her stockings still saturated with her fallen husband's blood.

"I'm Just a Patsy!"

After Oswald was taken to the Dallas police headquarters, arresting officers told detectives they had in custody the man who had killed Officer Tippit. Police found two forms of

identification on the suspect, one identifying him as Lee Oswald, the other said Alek J. Hidell, an alias often used by Oswald.

Later, as police were transferring Oswald to another part of the jail for questioning, the suspect was led through a room filled with reporters frantically shouting questions at him. Oswald, who had not yet been charged with Kennedy's murder, seemed surprised by the reception. When asked if he killed the president, Oswald said that no one had charged him with that yet, and in fact, the first time he had heard of such a charge was from the assembled reporters. As Oswald was led from the room, he indicated that he believed he had been set up to take the blame for the Kennedy assassination, yelling "I'm just a patsy!"[8]

Vice President Lyndon Johnson takes the oath of office in the cabin of Air Force One *as a dazed Jacqueline Kennedy (right) looks on.*

Interrogating Oswald

Government authorities have always insisted that they never made any written or audio record of their interrogation of Oswald after Kennedy's murder. This was extremely unorthodox according to New Orleans district attorney Jim Garrison. In his book *On the Trail of the Assassins* Garrison discusses this point:

> The Dallas Police Department, which closed its books on the case almost immediately . . . conducted a highly irregular inquiry. For example, after his arrest Lee Harvey Oswald was questioned while in the custody of Captain Will Fritz, head of the Dallas Police Homicide Division. As a prosecutor, I knew that recording of such questioning is routine even in minor felony cases. Yet . . . the alleged murderer of the President of the United States had been questioned . . . without any taping or short-hand notes by a stenographer. Nor was any attorney present. . . . This could not be mere sloppiness, I realized. A police officer of 30 years' experience like Captain Fritz had to be aware that anything Oswald said under such circumstances would be inadmissible in any subsequent trial. . . .

The more I read, the clearer it became that all the official government investigations of the assassination had systematically ignored any evidence that might lead to a conclusion other than that Lee Oswald was the lone assassin.

Lee Harvey Oswald speaks with reporters on his way to jail.

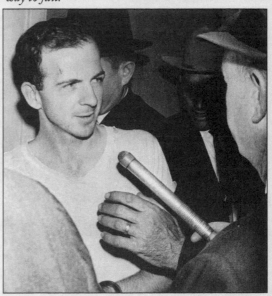

Oswald was finally led to an interrogation room where he underwent intense questioning by city, state, and federal authorities. Although Dallas police captain Will Fritz took notes during his initial interviews, no known notes, tape recordings, or films were made during twelve hours of FBI interrogation.

Killing the Suspect

The next day, Saturday, November 23, as a shocked nation mourned its fallen president, the FBI began releasing dozens of facts concerning Oswald's unusual background. After serving in the marines from 1957 to 1959, he defected to the Soviet Union, where he lived for several years. He then returned to the United States with a Russian wife, Marina, and the couple soon had two children. Although he had not finished high school, Oswald spoke fluent Russian.

In the months before Kennedy's assassination the suspect spent many hours handing out pro-Communist flyers on a street corner in New Orleans. In addition, a short time before the assassination, Oswald traveled to Mexico City, where he went to the Cuban consulate and indicated an intense desire to travel to Cuba and Russia.

These facts led investigating officers to conclude that Lee Harvey Oswald was a Communist whose political beliefs had inspired the murder of the president of the United States. Some suspected that Oswald might even have been working in league with spies from Cuba, the Soviet Union, or some other entity.

Oswald would never get the chance to publicly explain his actions, however. Two days after Kennedy's murder, on November 24, authorities decided to move the suspect from the city jail to the more secure county jail. At about 11:20 A.M., the handcuffed prisoner, flanked by several police detectives, was led through the basement of Dallas City Hall toward a waiting armored car. Despite the heavy security, nightclub owner Jack Ruby (born Jacob Rubenstein) leaped out of the crowd and shot Oswald in the stomach with a .38-caliber revolver. Unlike Kennedy's assassination, this event was captured on live television. And since all three major networks had suspended regular programming—and all commercials—to broadcast the breaking news, an estimated 175 million people—93 percent of all Americans—witnessed the shooting that Sunday afternoon.

In the aftermath of the shooting, Oswald was conscious for a few moments. Sensing this might be the last chance to talk to the suspect, Detective Billy Combest tried to communicate with Oswald:

I got right down on the floor with him, just literally on my hands and knees. And I asked him if he would like to make any confession, any statement in connection with the assassination of the President. . . . Several times he responded to me by shaking his head [side to side] in a definitive manner. . . . He wasn't going to correspond with me, he wasn't going to say anything.[9]

Oswald was taken to Parkland Memorial Hospital where the same doctors who had tried to save President Kennedy now tried to save his accused assassin. Those efforts were also futile and Oswald died at 1:07 P.M. He was buried on November 25 in Dallas the same day Kennedy was laid to rest in Arlington National Cemetery in Virginia.

The Warren Report

In the aftermath of the assassination, Oswald's ties to Cuba and the Soviet Union were publicized widely in the press. Many Americans—70 percent in one poll—said they believed that Oswald had not acted alone. And if Kennedy's assassination was planned or supported by an enemy foreign power, the murder of the president was an act of war.

In order to quell rumors and fears, President Johnson issued Executive Order No. 11130 to empower a blue-ribbon presidential commission to investigate Kennedy's assassination. It was headed by Supreme Court chief justice Earl Warren, and so named the Warren Commission. Members of the commission included recently fired CIA director Allen Dulles, future president Gerald Ford, then a Michigan congressman, and future senator Arlen Specter. None of the commission members had previous investigative experience and they did not hire outside investigators. Instead they relied solely on the findings of the FBI and CIA to draw their conclusions.

Even with these respected government leaders in charge of the investigation, answers to questions surrounding the murder seemed elusive, prompting Warren to say: "We may never know the full story in our lifetime."[10] In addition, the commission was under pressure by Johnson to produce a report quickly, before the upcoming presidential election in November 1964.

The Warren Commission operated entirely in secret and only visited Dallas briefly. On September 27, 1964, the commissioners released the *Report of the Warren Commission on the Assassination of President Kennedy*, commonly referred to as the Warren Report. It consists of a hefty twenty-six volumes of evidence and testimony plus a 726-page summary that reaches the following conclusions:

• Lee Harvey Oswald shot President Kennedy with a Mannlicher-Carcano rifle from the sixth-floor sniper's nest in the Texas School Book Depository.

Chief Justice Earl Warren turns over to President Johnson one of the twenty-six volumes comprising the Warren Commission investigation of Kennedy's assassination.

• The president was hit by the second and third of the three shots fired by Oswald, the third killing him. The shot that wounded Governor Connally was the second shot that had first passed through the president's back and throat.

• Oswald also killed Officer Tippit about forty-five minutes after the assassination.

• Oswald was himself murdered by Jack Ruby whose motive was to spare Jacqueline Kennedy the pain of having to return to Dallas to testify in Oswald's trial.

The Warren Report concludes: "The Commission found no evidence that either Lee Harvey Oswald or Jack Ruby was part of any conspiracy, domestic or foreign, to assassinate President Kennedy. . . . On the basis of the evidence before the Commission it concludes that Oswald acted alone."[11]

A Conspiracy Industry

As soon as the report was released, nearly every major newspaper and national magazine endorsed its conclusions. Reporters and editorial writers who doubted the Warren Report and publicized alternative conclusions were labeled agitators, "conspiracy buffs," and even enemies of the United States. As the *New York Times* editor Harrison Salisbury wrote: "Frequently these [alternate] theories . . . have the objective of undermining the United States. . . . Some have been aimed at sowing distrust and confusion at home. Others seek to convey to foreign countries the image of a violent America, helpless in the face of dangerous forces."[12]

Despite widespread media support some influential people questioned the commission's conclusions almost immediately. Robert Kennedy, the president's brother, was among them. He stated that he had "serious reservations about the Warren Commission Report [and] . . . was open to the possibilities of a conspiracy."[13]

Eerie Assassination Quirks

Almost as soon as Kennedy was shot in Dallas, people began to compare his assassination with that of Abraham Lincoln. And for those who believe Lee Harvey Oswald shot Kennedy, several mysterious coincidences surround each murder. The following are posted on "The Lincoln/Kennedy Coincidences" website:

The 100 Years Link:

Lincoln was elected President in 1860, while Kennedy was elected President in 1960.

Lincoln's successor—Andrew Johnson—was born in 1808, while Kennedy's successor—Lyndon Johnson—was born in 1908.

Lincoln's killer—John Wilkes Booth—was born in 1839, while Kennedy's killer—Lee Harvey Oswald—was born in 1939.

The Names:

The names Lincoln and Kennedy each contain seven letters.

Lincoln's secretary was [named] Kennedy, while Kennedy's secretary was [named] Lincoln.

Lincoln's and Kennedy's successors both had the surname Johnson.

The names Andrew Johnson and Lyndon Johnson each contain thirteen letters.

The names John Wilkes Booth and Lee Harvey Oswald each contain fifteen letters.

The Killings:

Lincoln and Kennedy were both killed on a Friday.

Both were killed in the presence of their wives.

Both were shot from behind and in the head.

Booth shot Lincoln in a theatre and hid in a warehouse, while Oswald shot Kennedy from a warehouse and hid in a theatre.

Both assassins were killed before being brought to trial.

Civil Rights:

Lincoln and Kennedy were both directly concerned with Civil Rights.

Booth and Oswald were both Southerners favoring unpopular ideas.

In the years following the release of the Warren Report, thousands of critics in the medical, scientific, legal, governmental, and law enforcement communities have questioned nearly every paragraph of the twenty-seven-volume report. The first published criticism of the Warren Report hit bookstands in 1966 when attorney Mark Lane released *Rush to Judgment*, which strongly denounces the Warren Commission, its secrecy, and its conclusions. Lane had not been convinced of Oswald's guilt and had tried to represent him before the commission. Although he was never able to do this, *Rush to Judgment* became the number one best-selling book of 1966 and has since sold over a million copies.

Since that time, conspiracy researchers have collectively written countless articles and more than two thousand books with provocative titles such as *High Treason* and *Killing Kennedy and the Hoax of the Century*. The mystery behind the murder deepened as conflicting theories placed the blame on suspects that included Mafia hit men, Secret Service, FBI and CIA agents, and even President Johnson. Author Gerald Posner offers his opinion as to why these books have been so successful:

> Besides skepticism over Oswald's murky background and his murder, strong psychological reasons prompted the public's early embrace of conspiracy theories. The notion that a misguided sociopath had wreaked such havoc made the crime seem senseless and devoid of political significance. By concluding that JFK was killed as a result of an elaborate plot, there is a belief that he died for a purpose, that a powerful group eliminated him for some critical issue.[14]

The various conspiracy theories have also been fueled by the government's refusal to release hundreds of thousands of documents pertaining to the event. By law, key elements of the investigation are locked away until the year 2039. That leaves the pubic with a tantalizing mystery. And for some the motives behind the murder of the martyred president remain an open question many decades after his death.

Chapter 2

How Many Bullets Were Fired?

One of the greatest controversies in the Kennedy assassination—and one that has generated the most debate— is how many bullets were fired and from which direction they came. The Warren Commission concludes that three bullets were fired at the presidential motorcade in little more than five seconds. Of those, only two hit the president. According to the Warren Report, the first missed the limousine completely, the second pierced Kennedy's throat "and most probably passed through the Governor's body,"[15] and the third was the head shot that killed Kennedy.

Many who read this account, and some who later investigated the circumstances of the shooting, found the three-bullet scenario beyond credibility. One of the clearest arguments against the three-bullet theory is the Warren Commission's own tests that found it would have been exceedingly difficult for Oswald to fire his rifle three times during the 5.6 seconds in which the president was killed. The commissioners hired three expert marksmen to test Oswald's Mannlicher-Carcano and found that only one marksman was able to fire three shots in less than 5.6 seconds. Other marksmen required from 6.45 to 8.25 seconds. And in six separate tests, none of the experts was able to hit the head or the neck of the target from the distance Oswald is said to have killed Kennedy during that time frame.

The commissioners also took testimony from witnesses who reported hearing more than three shots fired that day. According to the Warren Report "some . . . testified that they heard four and perhaps as many as five or six shots."[16]

Gerald Posner disputes such claims, saying that two hundred witnesses, or 88 percent of those who testified, heard only three shots. Experts who study acoustics also point out that Dealey Plaza is located in a "canyon" surrounded by the triple underpass and tall brick and concrete buildings which could have caused the echoes of gunfire to reverberate throughout the area. This was affirmed by a later study in which 178 witnesses were questioned. Forty-four percent said they were unable to pinpoint the direction of the gunfire, while 28 percent said it came from the School Book Depository, and 12 percent said it came from elsewhere. Like so much else in the Kennedy mystery, however, these statistics are hotly disputed and debated by critics.

The Single-Bullet Theory

Of the three bullets that the commissioners say were fired at the president, the second bullet has generated the most contentious debate. The Warren Report states that this bullet, known as Commission Exhibit 399, or CE 399, caused eight separate, nonfatal wounds in both Kennedy and Connally. Warren commissioner Arlen Specter describes the route of the bullet, saying that CE 399 entered Kennedy's back, exited his throat, hit Governor Connally by the right armpit, fractured his rib, punctured his lung, exited his chest, hit him in the right wrist, and then buried itself in his left thigh. At Parkland Memorial Hospital, the bullet allegedly fell out of Connally's thigh and onto his stretcher. The Warren Report states that a hospital worker found the bullet on Connally's stretcher.

Where Was the Press?

President Kennedy was assassinated before the invention of quality point-and-shoot cameras, video cameras, portable tape recorders, cell phones, and twenty-four-hour news coverage—a time when it was possible to kill the president of the United States in broad daylight in front of thousands of people with little clear recorded evidence.

At the time, only members of the press had the equipment necessary to record the event. And conspiracy researchers have long questioned the placement of the press car in the motorcade, eight vehicles behind the president. On every earlier occasion, reporters had ridden on a flatbed truck in front of the presidential limousine so that the camera crews could snap pictures and film the president from a clear angle as he waved to the crowds. Why they were not in place on November 22 remains a mystery but if the photographers were in their normal place in the motorcade, there would have been ample photographic, audio, and filmed records of the Kennedy assassination. Since this was not the case, many questions about the shooting remained unanswered.

Many who followed the investigation have openly questioned Specter's "single-bullet theory" and have asked how this one projectile could inflict so much damage. The bullet, they contend, would have had to change course several times and move in a manner that defies physics and logic. To create these wounds CE 399 would have had to exit Kennedy's neck, stop in midair, turn to the right, move over eighteen inches, stop again, and then continue on its way through Connally's back. After exiting Connally's body, CE 399 would have had to move downward, go through the right wrist, and somehow jog over from his right wrist to the left thigh. In *Rush to Judgment* Mark Lane dubbed this projectile the "magic bullet."[17]

One of the other problems with the single-bullet scenario is the physical condition of CE 399, which conspiracy researchers describe as "pristine," that is, visibly perfect. According to the testimony of experts who appeared before the Warren Commission, any bullet that passed through the bone and tissue of two people would be flattened, distorted, and broken apart. As Irving Shaw, a former army surgeon

An Associated Press wirephoto of the "magic bullet" shows its pristine condition.

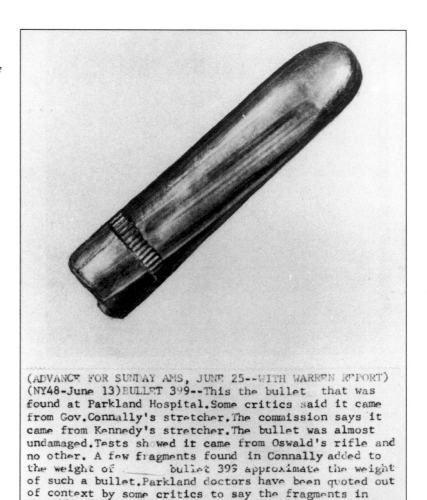

(ADVANCE FOR SUNDAY AMS, JUNE 25--WITH WARREN REPORT) (NY48--June 13)BULLET 399--This the bullet that was found at Parkland Hospital.Some critics said it came from Gov.Connally's stretcher.The commission says it came from Kennedy's stretcher.The bullet was almost undamaged.Tests showed it came from Oswald's rifle and no other. A few fragments found in Connally added to the weight of _____ bullet 399 approximate the weight of such a bullet.Parkland doctors have been quoted out of context by some critics to say the fragments in Connally are too big to have come from Bullet 399. (APWirephoto)(b31945fls)67

who had treated over one thousand shooting wounds, told Specter: "I feel that there would be some difficulty in explaining all of the wounds as being inflicted by bullet Exhibit 399 without causing more in the way of loss of substance to the bullet or deformation of the bullet."[18]

In later years, experts contradicted Shaw's testimony and lent more credence to the single-bullet theory. In 1976–1977, during a congressional investigation into the shooting, the House Select Committee on Assassinations (HSCA) addressed this issue, noting that the bullet was steel-jacketed and could have caused the eight wounds without getting too distorted in shape. As the HSCA report states, the bullet was a "long, stable, fully jacketed bullet, typical of ammunition often used by the military. Such ammunition tends to pass through body tissue more easily than soft nose hunting bullets [while still maintaining their original shape]."[19]

The Zapruder Film

Those who support the single-bullet theory—and those who disagree with it—have relied heavily on another piece

Shooting Down the Lone Gunman Theory

In *UFOs, JFK, and Elvis* conspiracy theorist Richard Belzer lists five reasons many believe that the Warren Commission's theory of the lone gunman shooting only three bullets at Kennedy is faulty:

1. There is . . . photographic and medical evidence that the fatal bullet was fired from the front of the president's car. . . . Since Oswald could only be in one place at a time and since we are to believe that he was happily ensconced in the Book Depository behind Kennedy, a second shooter would have to have fired the final bullet.

2. Test bullets were scarred and damaged after a single shot. Despite the convoluted path theoretically traveled by the "magic bullet," the bullet identified by the Warren Commission as the projectile that passed through Connally and Kennedy was notably undamaged. In fact, according to Aubrey Bell, attending nurse at Parkland Memorial Hospital, more lead was removed from

Connally's wrist than is missing from the "magic bullet."

3. The "magic bullet" would have to have been fired by a similarly "magic rifle." Experts agree that a high-precision semi-automatic weapon would be necessary to repeatedly hit a moving target from the distance of the Book Depository. Oswald's gun was not a sharpshooting weapon, but a rifle with a misaligned scope.

4. A maximum of 1.8 seconds elapsed between the moment Kennedy was first hit and the fatal shot. Since the bolt of Oswald's Mannlicher-Carcano rifle could not be operated in less than 2.3 seconds, it couldn't possibly have been the sole murder weapon.

5. Dignitaries in the president's motorcade reported that they smelled gunpowder. It is unlikely that the smell of gunpowder would travel to ground zero from the sixth-floor window of the Book Depository, a building dozens of yards away.

of evidence used by the Warren Commission: an 8-mm motion picture known as the Zapruder film. Like the pristine bullet, this short film is also steeped in controversy.

The Zapruder film was taken by Abraham Zapruder, a New York executive living in Dallas who took time off work to see President Kennedy as his motorcade passed Dealey Plaza. Zapruder was standing on the grassy knoll recording the scene with his new Bell & Howell 8-mm movie camera as shots rang out and the president was killed. Incredibly, Zapruder's twenty-six shocking seconds of grainy color film are the clearest photographic record of Kennedy's murder. As *Life* magazine stated: "Of all the witnesses to the tragedy, the only unimpeachable one is the 8-mm movie camera of Abraham Zapruder."[20]

Unfortunately, such cameras do not record sound, so investigators could not hear how many shots were fired or how far apart they were. But the Zapruder film does show the head shot that killed the president and also shows other details of the shooting. Most important, the Zapruder film provides investigators with a sort of time clock of the assassination. The Bell & Howell camera shot movie film at a rate of 18.8 frames per second. At twenty-six seconds in length, this yielded 488.8 frames in all. Of those, approximately 105 frames actually capture the assassination. The Warren Commission divided that number by 18.8, and determined that the assassination took place in about 5.6 seconds. They also used individual frames in attempts to determine exactly when each shot was fired.

Even as it provides this important information the Zapruder film does not tell the complete story of the assassination. For example, Kennedy's limousine passes behind a freeway sign and is blocked from the view of the camera at frame 210. When the limo emerges from behind the sign at frame 225, Kennedy is already reacting to being shot by grabbing his throat with both hands. This left the Warren Commission to conclude "the President was probably shot through the neck between frames 210 and 225."[21]

The Curious Life of the Zapruder Film

It has been said that the camera does not lie, but in the case of the Zapruder film, conspiracy theorists believe this is not necessarily true. Like almost every other aspect of the Kennedy assassination, strange and curious events surround the film that is the clearest known record of the murder.

After the assassination, Abraham Zapruder made copies of the film. The original film was given to Secret Service agents who flew it to Washington to be analyzed by the National Photographic Interpretations Center. Some people suggest that the government altered that film. The original film, they said, showed blood and brains coming out of the back of Kennedy's head during the fatal shot, and this apparently is not seen in later prints of the film.

Zapruder kept one copy for himself and sold a copy to *Life* magazine for $250,000

the day after the shooting. *Life* published several still frames of the film, although not frames 314 to 320 that purport to show the president's backward motion at the fatal head shot.

After this point, the Zapruder film more or less disappeared from the public for twelve years. Americans did not see the complete movie of Kennedy's murder until 1975. When it was shown on television, millions of people came to believe that Kennedy was shot from the front because of the way the president's skull and blood sprayed to the rear. Conspiracy researchers believe that if the entire Zapruder film would have been made public in the months after the assassination, it would have proved that someone other than Oswald killed the president.

If the Warren Commission had stopped there, the matter of when the president was shot might have been settled. But the commission muddled its own conclusion when it added that "a victim of a bullet wound may not react immediately and, in some situations . . . the victim may not even know where he has been hit, or when."[22] This indicates that Kennedy may have been reacting from a shot fired even before frame 210. Such contradictions and ambiguities opened the door to numerous theories and interpretations. However, while the exact moment of impact is unclear, the Warren Report relied on the Zapruder film for its conclusion that only three shots were fired.

Three, Six, or More Bullets?

Like so many other aspects of the Kennedy assassination, even the Zapruder film has introduced new questions and has been open to a wide range of interpretations. For example, while the Warren Commission used the film to conclude that three shots were fired at the president, conspiracy researchers say that it shows as many as six shots were fired that day in Dealey Plaza.

Most conspiracy theorists say that frame 150 of the film shows the president turning to his right and looking at the grassy knoll. At this point he allegedly hears the first shot fired, the one that the Warren Commission says missed the car. At this time, critics say, the president's limo would not have been visible from Oswald's sniper's nest on the sixth floor of the School Book Depository because an oak tree blocked the view. The first shot so startled Zapruder, however, that the film can be seen blurring as his hand jumped in reaction.

The president continued to wave until shot number two pierced his throat. Although the Warren Report says the second shot was fired by Oswald from behind, critics say frames 188 through 191 of the Zapruder film seem to show the president's body pushed rearward by the force of the bullet. They contend that this proves shot two came from the front, either from the grassy knoll or the top of the triple underpass. At this point, the limousine disappears from view behind a highway sign, but when it emerges on frame 228, the president is clearly clutching his throat with both hands.

A third shot, say conspiracy researchers, was fired at almost the same time as the second. This missed Kennedy and hit Governor Connally. At this time, the Zapruder film clearly shows Connally holding his white Stetson cowboy hat in his right hand. Some who have studied the film claim that it would have been impossible for the governor to hang onto his hat if he was also shot through the wrist by this bullet.

Researchers have traced the trajectory of the bullet as it passed through Connally's body. They conclude that this alleged third shot did come from the School Book Depository but from the southwest corner, opposite from

Oswald's sniper's nest. Some researchers and witnesses say this shot came from the fourth or fifth floor.

A fourth shot is said to have struck Kennedy in the middle of his back, six inches below the shoulder. This bullet might have been fired from the second-floor window of the Dal-Tex Building on Elm east of the School Book Depository. Outside researchers say this is the Warren Commission's "magic bullet," the one that supposedly went through the president's throat and struck Connally. The president's personal physician, Admiral George G. Burkley, has described a wound in the middle of Kennedy's upper back, and a photograph of the president's suit coat clearly shows a bullet hole in this area. The Warren Commission, however, believed this shot had exited from Kennedy's throat because he was slumped over. Conspiracy researchers contend that the Zapruder film contradicts this finding.

Many conspiracy theorists challenge the findings of the Warren Commission, whose seven members are pictured here.

Shot from the Grassy Knoll?

Outside researchers believe a fifth shot is actually the one that killed the president. They believe frame 313 shows that shot hitting him in the right temple and leaving a hole the size of a fist in his head. This shot has also generated its share of controversy. Researchers contend that the Zapruder film clearly shows Kennedy's body thrown back and to the left as if the shot came from the grassy knoll, ahead and to his right.

Tourists visit the grassy knoll in late 1963 to pay their respects to the slain president. The Texas School Book Depository looms in the background.

When the HSCA looked into this issue, it reached conflicting conclusions. Michael Baden, head of the committee's forensic pathology panel, concluded that "nerve damage from a bullet entering [the front of] the President's head could have caused his back muscles to tighten which, in turn, could have caused his head to move toward the rear . . . [and] the rearward movement of the President's head would not be fundamentally inconsistent with a bullet striking from the rear."[23]

Others disagree, however, and this issue has never been resolved. But as Dr. Gary Aguilar writes in James H. Fetzer's book *Murder in Dealey Plaza:* "Any bullet striking JFK at the base of his skull from Oswald's supposed perch would have created a 'blow-out' exit wound in JFK's face . . . including a good portion of the right forehead, the entire right eye socket, and part of the cheekbone."[24] This sort of wound was never received by the president.

Those who believe that there were two shooters also say that a sixth shot came about a half second after the fifth. Shot six, said to be fired from the same window in the School Book Depository as number three, hit Connally, shattering his right wrist and exiting into his thigh. The governor reacted to this shot by dropping his Stetson hat.

Some researchers believe that at least two more shots were fired at the presidential motorcade as indicated by two bullet marks that were found in streets in the area. The trajectory of one bullet left a long streak on a manhole cover in Dealey Plaza. The trajectory of this shot suggests that it came from the Dallas Records Building on Houston Street.

If all these shots were fired, as conspiracy theorists say, then there must have been at least two assassins at work in Dealey Plaza—and maybe more. And none of the shots seem to have come from Oswald's sniper's nest in the School Book Depository.

Some take the two-assassin theory even further and make the shocking claim that Secret Service agents were in on the plot to kill the president. As proof, they point to the inaction of the agents even as shots rained down on the motorcade. As Warren Report critic Richard Belzer writes in *UFOs, JFK, and Elvis:*

> As researchers have documented . . . photos taken at the time of the shooting show a bizarre lack of reaction from the agents riding behind Kennedy. While the president grasps his throat, Secret Service agents are looking around—two toward the rear and two toward Kennedy. With the exception of Clint Hill, an agent brought in at the last minute by the First Lady, they make no move to shield the president from further gunfire. Most peculiar, after the first shot is fired, Kennedy's driver, Secret Service Agent William Greer, actually brings the car to a halt. Though he testified that he kept the Lincoln moving between twelve and fifteen miles per hour at all times, films clearly show the car slowing to nearly a standstill until the fatal bullet hits its mark.[25]

What the Witnesses Said

Witnesses who stated that the Secret Service failed to react as the president was shot were ignored by the Warren Commission. Critics charge that the commissioners also refused to hear testimony from forty people who saw Kennedy's fatal head shot delivered from the front. Typical of these witnesses is Jean Hill who stated: "I saw a man fire from behind the wooden fence. I saw a puff of smoke and some sort of movement from the grassy knoll." County surveyor Robert West, whose job required him to carefully scrutinize land boundaries, said the shots came "from the northwest quadrant of Dealey Plaza—the area of the picket fence on the grassy knoll." A retired U.S. Air Force major, an expert in weapons and gunshots, said "I saw blood going to the rear and left. . . . That doesn't happen if the bullet came from the Depository." Others support the theory that shots were also fired from the School Book Depository, but not from the sixth-floor sniper's nest. Factory worker Carolyn Walther said: "I glanced up at the Depository Building. There were two men in the corner window on the fourth or fifth floor. One man . . . held a rifle with the barrel pointed downward [at Kennedy]. I thought he was some kind of guard."[26]

Immediately after the shooting, others who took photographs of the incident claim they were accosted by unidentified men. Beverly Oliver, a nightclub singer, was standing on the other side of the street from the picket fence when Kennedy was shot. She was filming the scene with a brand new movie camera and had a clear view of the grassy knoll. (Because of the scarf she was wearing around her head, she is

Four Shots Heard on Tape

In 1978 government investigators working for the House Select Committee on Assassinations analyzed a police tape, called a dictabelt recording, that had been made when an unidentified motorcycle policeman who was escorting Kennedy's motorcade left his microphone on by accident. By using computers, scientists were able to develop a model of the unique acoustic properties of the grassy knoll. Using this "acoustic fingerprint" they were able to determine with considerable accuracy that four shots were fired at Kennedy that day. As Bob Callahan writes in *Who Shot JFK? A Guide to the Major Conspiracy Theories*:

The grassy knoll shot was there all right. From its fingerprint, the scientists were able

to deduce within a margin of error of plus or minus one and a half feet the exact location of the microphone which had recorded the shot. This location corresponded exactly to where the Dallas police had at the time already located the motorcycle in question. The two scientists then reached an even more astounding conclusion. The acoustic fingerprint located the grassy knoll gunman within a margin of error of plus or minus five feet in circumference at the exact point behind the wooden fence where [railroad worker] Lee Bowers had once seen an unidentified man standing . . . and his five railroad co-workers had seen a puff of smoke rise in the seconds after the actual shooting.

known to conspiracy researchers as the "babushka lady.") Oliver says she saw Kennedy's head shot and saw a figure and a puff of smoke from behind the picket fence. After the assassination, the FBI contacted Oliver at work and took her film which, mysteriously, was never seen again.

In addition to Oliver, a young serviceman, Gordon Arnold, was shooting a home movie of the president from the grassy knoll with his back to the picket fence. Arnold, who had just finished live-fire training exercises in the military, says he was startled to hear and feel a bullet whiz by his head. The young serviceman quickly dropped to the ground and claimed a second shot passed directly over him. After this shot found its target, a man in a policeman's uniform, but with dirty hands and no hat, approached the young soldier. Arnold stated that the mysterious policeman was shaking and crying and holding a rifle in his hand. This man purportedly kicked Arnold, grabbed his camera, yanked out the film, and threw it on the ground. Gerald Posner disputes this story, writing: "The problem is that it appears Arnold was not even at Dealey Plaza on the day of the assassination. People on the grassy knoll near where Arnold says he was are clearly visible in the pictures taken of the knoll. Although Arnold claims he is not visible because he is lying flat on the ground, photo enhancement shows no such person."[27]

Mary Ann Moorman, however, can prove she was on Dealey Plaza when the president was killed. Moorman was standing across the street from the grassy knoll and managed to click a Polaroid picture one-sixth of a second before Kennedy's fatal head shot. In 1995 photographic researchers studying the photograph claimed they could see the man dressed as a policeman mentioned by Arnold. Known as "Badgeman" because of the police badge on his chest, this grainy figure appears to be holding a rifle—and a puff of smoke is seen coming out of the barrel. Conspiracy theorists speculate that Badgeman fired the fatal shot that killed Kennedy and was dressed as a policeman in order to blend into the crowd.

The Mysterious Witness Deaths

In the twelve years following the JFK assassination, eighteen material witnesses met with peculiar, often violent deaths. In later years, more than one hundred met tragic ends. At least twelve associates of Ruby died soon after the murder. Those who think that there was a conspiracy to kill Kennedy believe that these witnesses may have been murdered to prevent the plot from being exposed.

The most mysterious story is that of stripper Rose Cherami who was thrown out of a speeding auto and left to die on November 20, 1963, by mobsters working for Ruby. Cherami lived, however, and spent the next two days telling hospital workers that Kennedy was going to be killed in Dallas. She was dismissed as a lunatic until Kennedy was murdered two days later. Although she was interviewed by authorities after the assassination, she was not believed to be a credible witness because she was a heroin addict. In September 1965 Cherami was mysteriously killed when her head was run over by a car while she was lying on the side of a road in Texas.

The most prominent person killed in relation to the Kennedy assassination was Dorothy Kilgallen, a reporter and popular TV game show celebrity. Kilgallen was the only reporter to be granted an interview with Ruby and she claimed to have a thick file that she said would expose a conspiracy behind the Kennedy assassination. In November 1965 Kilgallen was found dead in her apartment. The file was missing, and Kilgallen, who was not a known alcoholic or drug user, was found to have enough barbiturates in her system to kill ten men. Doctors ruled her death a suicide.

Reporter Dorothy Kilgallen, who claimed to have proof of a conspiracy behind the assassination, died under suspicious circumstances.

These barely visible figures, blown up from a piece of photographic film less than one-tenth of an inch square, are open to interpretation. Disputing the existence of Badgeman, Gerald Posner writes that in order to shoot over the five-foot-high picket fence next to the colonnade on the grassy knoll, Badgeman "would have been completely exposed at the rear, making it impossible to fire from that location without being seen by witnesses. In addition to more than a dozen who could have seen such a shooter, three witnesses were only a few feet in front of the fence, and they never saw anyone behind the fence."[28]

Contradicting Posner, Lee Bowers, who worked in a railroad switching tower behind the grassy knoll, said that he did see Badgeman near the picket fence both before and after the assassination. Bowers died about two years later under mysterious circumstances in a one-car accident.

Critics claim that when Bowers told the Warren Commission he could identify the man who shot Kennedy from the grassy knoll, his evidence was ignored. So too were the stories of dozens of other witnesses, including Arnold and Moorman, who smelled gunsmoke and heard shots while standing on Dealey Plaza. (If the shots were fired from the School Book Depository, witnesses would not have been able to smell gunsmoke on the street.)

By ignoring these witnesses, some say the commissioners have inadvertently encouraged conspiracy theorists to continue their quest to formulate theories about events in Dealey Plaza that dark day in Dallas. And with so many conflicting and confusing statements, it seems as if the mystery may never be solved.

Chapter 3

Who Was Oswald and Did He Kill the President?

As the central character in the Kennedy assassination Lee Harvey Oswald has become an enigma in the decades since his death. Hundreds of books and articles—and several Hollywood movies—have questioned Oswald's complicity in the murder. And the intense scrutiny of his life and activities before the shooting have only intensified the mystery of who Oswald was and whether he killed the president.

Although he was only twenty-four years old when he died, Oswald's life was marked by contradictions and conflicts. In the six years before he died, he served honorably in the U.S. Marine Corps, then defected to the Soviet Union. When he returned to the United States he publicly promoted Communist propaganda and was also seen in the company of staunch anti-Communists. Along the way, Oswald is said to have had contact with military intelligence, the FBI, the CIA, and the Mafia. With such a twisted maze of associations and connections, it is little wonder that Oswald's life has been the focus of speculation, conjecture, and mystery.

Strange Behavior

Oswald's life in the weeks just before Kennedy's assassination was remarkably uneventful. Six weeks before the president was killed on the streets of Dallas, Oswald was unemployed and searching for a job. He was finally hired to fill orders at the Texas School Book Depository at $1.25 an hour.

During the workweek Oswald did not live with his Russian-born wife Marina and two young daughters, but rather paid seven dollars a week to stay at a rooming house about four miles from his new job. He was registered there under the pseudonym O.H. Lee, a reversal of his real name.

Lee Harvey Oswald spent weeknights at this Dallas rooming house, where he had registered under an assumed name.

When questioned about this pseudonym by Dallas police, Oswald said: "My landlady didn't understand my name correctly, so it was her idea to call me O.H. Lee."[29] While living at the boardinghouse, according to his landlady Gladys Johnson, Oswald had no visitors, spoke to no one when coming and going, and spent 95 percent of the time in his room.

Oswald stayed with his family on weekends. They lived outside Dallas with a woman named Ruth Paine. Paine had helped Oswald obtain the job at the School Book Depository by calling on a few friends who worked there. Oswald spent his weekends playing with his children and watching football on television.

Oswald did not know how to drive a car and often rode to the Paine residence with Buell Frazier, a coworker, who lived a few houses away from Ruth Paine. On the Thursday before Kennedy's assassination, Oswald made an unusual weekday visit to Paine's house, saying that he needed to pick up some curtains that Marina had made for him. Paine said he was even quieter than usual and overslept the next morning.

On November 22, 1963, Oswald left his wedding ring and wallet behind in his room, and then caught a ride to work with Frazier. When he got in the car, Oswald laid a package down in the backseat. It was wrapped in a brown paper bag. When Frazier asked what it was, Oswald told him it was curtain rods. The Warren Commission says that in reality this parcel contained the disassembled Mannlicher-Carcano rifle Oswald used to kill Kennedy.

As with many other aspects of the assassination mystery, there are conflicting stories. When FBI agents first questioned Frazier, he insisted that the package was twenty-seven inches long, about eight inches shorter than a disassembled Mannlicher-Carcano. When questioned years later, Frazier admitted it might have been longer, saying "I only glanced at [the package,] . . . hardly paid attention to it."[30] Then in 1978 Frazier told an interviewer that Oswald walked into work holding one end of the package in his hand with the other end tucked up under his armpit. If the thirty-eight-inch rifle was in the package, Oswald's arms were not long enough to allow him to carry it in this manner. Whatever the case, the FBI found a brown paper bag on the sixth floor of the School Book Depository. This bag has Oswald's fingerprints on it and fibers inside that are from a blanket that had wrapped the weapon while it was stored in Ruth Paine's garage.

Oswald's Whereabouts in Question

There are also conflicting stories as to the whereabouts of Oswald immediately before and after the shooting. According to the Warren Report, Oswald's coworker Charles Givens saw the suspect on the sixth floor of the School Book Depository at about 11:55 A.M. Givens said to Oswald, "'Boy, are you going downstairs, it's almost lunchtime?' Oswald said, 'No sir.'"[31] This story is contradicted, however, by secretary Carolyn Arnold, who told *Conspiracy* author Anthony Summers that she observed Oswald at 12:15 sitting in the lunchroom on the second floor of the School Book Depository eating his lunch alone. Other witnesses who were in the lunchroom between 12:00 and 12:30 said they did not see Oswald.

When Dallas police officer Marion Baker raced to the School Book Depository immediately after Kennedy was shot, he and building manager Ray Truly saw Oswald standing alone in the lunchroom nonchalantly drinking a Coke. According to Baker, Oswald seemed calm and unaware of the tragedy that had unfolded on the street below. The time the officer noted was 12:32 P.M.—two minutes after the 12:30 shooting.

To be the shooter, Oswald would have had to squeeze out of the sniper's nest, walk through aisles cluttered with pallets of books, hide his rifle between several dozen boxes of books, and run down four flights of stairs to the lunchroom without anyone seeing him—all in just two minutes. The Warren Report states this is exactly what happened. Baker later retraced the route Oswald would have taken down the four flights of stairs and was able to make the journey to the lunchroom at a normal pace in one minute, eighteen seconds. Conspiracy researchers, however, doubt Baker's story and say that Oswald would have been disheveled and out of breath after such a sprint.

Was It Oswald's Gun?

Whether or not Oswald was on the sixth floor of the School Book Depository at the time of the shooting, after his arrest he steadfastly maintained his innocence. Oswald told the

Did Oswald Know the Parade Route?

The Warren Report says that Oswald shot Kennedy from the sixth floor of the Texas School Book Depository. But the motorcade route was changed at the last minute, and no one outside the president's circle should have had advanced knowledge that Kennedy's limousine would pass by the School Book Depository. This has prompted conspiracy researchers to wonder: Why would Oswald carry a rifle to work to shoot the president if, like everyone else, he thought the motorcade would be traveling down Main Street, out of the gunshot range of the School Book Depository? As conspiracy researcher Bob Callahan writes in *Who Shot JFK?*

[Unless] Oswald had been somehow in touch with the Dallas politicians who persuaded President Kennedy to change that route at the last minute, he would have left for work

that morning, curtain rod or rifle package in hand, knowing that the President's motorcade would come no closer than a block away from the School Book Depository. The map of the scheduled motorcade route which appeared in the *Dallas Morning News* on Nov. 22, 1963 clearly showed that the President was scheduled to travel directly down Main Street through the Triple Underpass . . . for his journey to the Trade Mart for lunch.

If someone had not persuaded the President to make a last minute double detour onto Houston Street, and then directly in front of the Book Depository onto Elm, it would have been impossible for Oswald, or anyone else, to have hit the President from the sixth floor of that building with a $14 mail-order rifle.

reporters at Dallas police headquarters: "I didn't kill anybody. . . . I haven't shot anybody. . . . What is this all about?"[32] Later, during initial interviews with authorities, police report that Oswald repeatedly asked for legal representation. And the only thing he would admit to was hitting a policeman in the mouth during the struggle before his arrest. Dallas police captain Will Fritz later said that Oswald told him: "I am not a malcontent. Nothing irritated me about the President."[33] Oswald repeatedly said he did not shoot anybody and the police never did obtain a signed confession.

Meanwhile the FBI and Dallas police could not positively tie the rifle to Oswald. Usually when a person fires a rifle, in addition to leaving fingerprints, he has traces of gunpowder on his face, fingers, or clothing that can be identified with tests. Investigators found no such conclusive evidence on Oswald. In addition, on Saturday November 23 the FBI announced that the rough fingerprints they found on the Mannlicher-Carcano were "insufficient for purposes of . . . identification . . . [and] were of no value."[34] On November 29, however, the FBI announced that it had found a palm print on the rifle.

In a more typical case, this probably would have ended speculation about who fired the fatal shots. But this case was far from typical. A statement by mortician Paul Grundy, who prepared Oswald's body for burial, raised a new set of questions. Grundy states that when FBI agents arrived at the funeral parlor, they took fingerprints from Oswald's lifeless body.

> And when they did come, they fingerprinted. And the only reason that we knew they did, they were carrying a satchel and equipment and asked us if they might have the preparation room to themselves. And after it was all over, we found ink on Lee Harvey's hands showing that they had fingerprinted him and palm-printed him. We had to take that ink back off in order to prepare him for burial.[35]

Word of this led to speculation that FBI agents planted the palm print under pressure from FBI director J. Edgar Hoover, who was eager to convict Oswald of the president's murder.

While the palm print remains a matter of debate, researchers eventually proved that the fingerprints on the gun belong to Oswald. In 1993 the *Frontline* program on PBS used modern scientific methods to analyze the prints. Researchers were able to clearly trace these partial fingerprints to Oswald. However, this new evidence simply proves that Oswald handled the rifle—it does not prove that he used it to kill the president.

Was Oswald a Secret Agent?

The physical evidence is but one piece of the assassination puzzle. There is also the matter of Oswald's private life which is a confusing mix of cowardice and bravado, ineptitude and achievement.

The Warren Report describes Oswald as a lonely loser, his life marked by unhappiness, frustration, and eventually, murderous rage against Kennedy. But since his death, Oswald's life has grown into one of the great mysteries in history, with dozens of twists and turns that baffle experts to this day.

Oswald was born in New Orleans in 1939 two months after his father died. Growing up, Oswald was often in trouble for petty offenses and has been described by investigators as someone who was emotionally disturbed. Oswald tried to join the marines when he was only sixteen. When he was rejected because of his age, he proceeded to memorize the entire *Marine Corps Manual* and finally joined the corps on his seventeenth birthday. During his three-year tour of duty in the marines, Oswald learned the skills of a sharpshooter. His inability to accurately shoot his rifle, however, earned him the nickname "Shitbird."

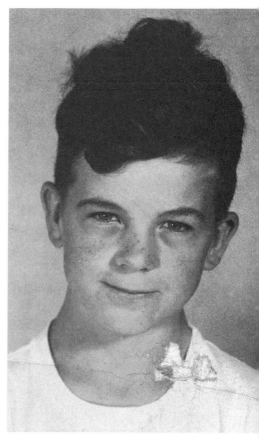

Oswald was an emotionally troubled boy, who often broke the law.

In addition to shooting, Oswald learned to operate radar equipment and was stationed at a military intelligence installation at Atsugi, Japan. This was also the base of one of the largest CIA stations in Asia, home to the Agency's chemical, biological, and physiological warfare experiments. Oswald's job at Atsugi was to monitor the flights of top-secret U2 spy planes photographing Soviet military installations from high in the sky.

In 1959 Oswald received an honorable discharge from the marines. Two weeks later—with only two hundred dollars in his pocket—the nineteen-year-old Oswald moved to the Soviet Union. This move took place at the height of the Cold War, a time of intense hostility between the Soviet Union and the United States.

No one really knows why Oswald went to the Soviet Union. The Warren Report states that he was unhappy with the United States and chose to defect to the Soviet Union in search of a better life. Others who have followed the case say Oswald may have gone to the Soviet Union to act as a spy for the U.S. government, pointing to several significant events to support that belief.

Oswald had been trained to speak Russian during his hitch in the marines. Since intelligence agents were ostensibly the only people given lessons in Russian, Oswald may have been trained as a spy. Whether or not this is true, at the time the State Department did run a program that placed phony defectors within the Soviet Union in order to conduct spying activities. Those who believe Oswald was groomed as a spy point to the fact that when he met his future wife, Marina Nikolaevna Prusakova, at a dancehall in Minsk, she thought he was a

As a marine, Oswald learned Russian, leading some to conclude that he was trained as a spy.

Soviet citizen because of the way he acted and because he was so fluent in her native language.

If Oswald was a spy posing as a defector, he did not fool Soviet secret police agents in the KGB who kept him under surveillance twenty-four hours a day. Suspicious of his motives, officials told Oswald he could not stay in the Soviet Union. Oswald reacted by slashing his wrists in a suicide attempt. Soviet psychiatrists evaluated the defector, determined that he was mentally unstable, but, for reasons unknown, let him remain in the country.

While recovering from his suicide attempt, Oswald decided to renounce his American citizenship. This act, and the events that followed, have led conspiracy researchers to believe that Oswald was given special treatment by the U.S. government that would have been highly unusual unless he was a spy.

According to former FBI agent and New Orleans district attorney Jim Garrison, Oswald,

> made a dramatic appearance at the American Embassy. He flamboyantly handed over his passport and a letter that concluded that his allegiance was with the Union of Soviet Socialist Republics [USSR]. He also announced he would give them information about the Marine Corps and the highly secret radar operations he had been involved in [at Atsugi].[36]

Such actions aiding an enemy government would have permanently disqualified most people from ever returning to the United States. Oswald, however, was allowed to return to the United States in May 1962 with his new wife Marina. This action was approved by the State Department, and the American embassy even lent him the money in a "repatriation loan," which can only be made, according to State Department regulations, if the recipient's "loyalty to the United States [has been established] beyond question."[37]

Any one of these events alone might not have resulted in suspicions that Oswald was a spy. Taken as a whole, however, they seem to many to show that Oswald was a secret agent working for the CIA or some branch of military intelligence.

Oswald the Revolutionary?

In August 1962 Oswald moved to Dallas where his puzzling behavior began to frighten his wife. According to the Warren Report, in late March 1963 Oswald asked Marina to photograph him striking a pose as a Communist revolutionary, dressed in black, wearing a pistol on his hip, holding a rifle in one hand and two Communist newspapers, the *Militant* and the *Worker*, in the other. Marina was reluctant to take what could be interpreted as incriminating photos, but relented after Oswald explained that he wanted to send one picture to the *Militant* and save the other for his daughter. When she asked him why their young daughter would want a photo of him holding guns, Oswald said, "To remember Papa by sometime."[38]

In the weeks after the photos were taken, Oswald's erratic behavior continued as he became obsessed with a popular right-wing leader, retired Major General Edwin A. Walker, who lived in Dallas. Walker, a staunch segregationist and anti-Communist, was a controversial figure who often gave speeches at meetings of right-wing political organizations such as the John Birch Society. Oswald compared Walker to World War II Nazi dictator Adolf Hitler.

According to testimony given to the Warren Commission by Marina, Oswald put Walker's home under surveillance and even took several photos of the back of his house. In the following weeks Oswald spent many hours studying maps of the neighborhood and the photos of Walker's house.

On April 10 Oswald left home with his Mannlicher-Carcano rifle and traveled to Walker's house. While he was

Phony Photos?

The authenticity of the photographs showing Oswald with his guns has been called into question over the years. Immediately after his arrest for Kennedy's murder Oswald himself denied that the photos were authentic. According to notes kept by Captain Will Fritz, Oswald became visibly agitated after looking at the pictures and said that someone had altered the photographs and pasted his face on someone else's body. In Oswald's words:

> That picture is not mine, but the face is mine. The picture has been made by superimposing my face. The other part of the picture is not me at all, and I have never seen this picture before. I understand photography real well, and . . . in time, I will be able to show you that is not my picture and that it has been made by someone else. . . . It was entirely possible that the Police Department has superimposed this part of the photograph over the body of someone else.

In the years after Oswald's death, photographic experts have studied these photos extensively, claiming that there are many oddities about the photos. The shadows in the photos seem to indicate that they were taken at different times of day. For example, there is a dark symmetrical shadow under Oswald's nose, suggesting the sun was directly overhead at around noon when the picture was taken. But Oswald's neck is dark on one side and light on the other, indicating that this part of the photo was taken around 10:00 A.M. when the sun was to the side. The shadow of his body extends far out behind the person in the photo and some say this is a shadow that would be produced around 4:00 P.M.

Oswald poses with his guns in this famous and controversial photo.

gone, Marina discovered the two backyard photos of Oswald along with a long note written in Russian. In it Oswald told Marina that he might not return home and that he paid the rent and utility bills. He told her she could survive for a month or two on his last paycheck from work, which would be waiting in a post office box. He also gave directions to the jail in case he was "taken prisoner."[39] Meanwhile, Oswald was observing Walker through the window of his house as the general prepared his income taxes at a desk in his dining room. Around 11 P.M., Oswald allegedly took a shot at Walker but a wooden window frame deflected the bullet and saved the general's life.

Oswald returned home panicky and shaken and told Marina what he had done. Although he was frightened that he would be arrested, news reports confirmed that the police had no suspects.

After Oswald's death, his wife Marina linked him to an attempt to murder Major General Edwin A. Walker.

Oswald was not connected to the shooting until after his death, and then only on the basis of testimony by Marina. With no witnesses and no conclusive evidence there are those who doubt Oswald was involved in the attempted murder of Walker. They allege that Marina, as a Russian immigrant, might have been pressured by the FBI to incriminate her deceased husband in order to make it appear that he was eager to gain notoriety through political assassination. The Warren Report makes this point, saying, "[Oswald had] a strong concern for his place in history. If the attack [on Walker] had succeeded and Oswald had been caught, the pictures showing him with a rifle and his Communist . . . newspapers would probably have appeared on the front pages of newspapers and magazines all over the country."[40]

The Cuban Conundrum

Whether or not Oswald tried to shoot Walker, one week later he left his family in Dallas and took up residence in New Orleans. He did not attempt to hide from authorities,

Oswald sought publicity by passing out pro–Castro handbills on the streets of New Orleans.

as might be expected after attempting murder. Instead Oswald tried very hard to become a public figure by flaunting his Communist sympathies.

First, Oswald took a minimum-wage job in New Orleans at the Reily Coffee Company. In his free time he managed a local chapter of the Fair Play for Cuba Committee (FPCC). The goals of this organization included restoring diplomatic, trade, and tourist relations with Cuba. These and other ties with Cuba had been cut off by the U.S. government after Castro gained control of the country. Oswald was the only member of the New Orleans chapter of the FPCC.

In August 1963 Oswald was often seen distributing pro-Castro handbills in front of the organization's office. This activity sometimes provoked vociferous arguments and even scuffles with passing Cuban exiles who were violently opposed to Castro. These confrontations were photographed several times by the press and, on one occasion, Oswald was arrested during an altercation for disturbing the peace. This publicity garnered Oswald an invitation to appear on a local radio show called *Conversation Carte Blanche,* in which he talked about his interest in communism, Cuba, and the Soviet Union.

Oswald's actions were highly unusual during this era of the Cold War, when Americans were almost unanimous in their fear and distrust of Communist governments. This behavior, however, seemed of little significance until Kennedy was shot. Investigators began to examine the activities of some of Oswald's neighbors.

Oswald's conspicuous support of communism was taking place very close to the offices of a man named Guy Banister, a former high-ranking FBI operative and a resolute anti-Communist. Banister spent much of his time recruiting anti-Castro Cuban exiles to train in secret CIA camps for another Bay-of-Pigs-type mission against Fidel Castro. The offices of Oswald and Banister were in the same building and on the same floor even though they had separate entrances. Banister's secretary Delphine Roberts said that she saw Oswald in Banister's office on several occasions. That the two men, one allegedly supporting Castro and the other working to kill the dictator, would have several meetings seems suspicious to some. Garrison believes that Oswald was not really a Communist but was asked to pose as one and that his activities "were designed to accomplish only one thing: to create a highly visible public profile for Lee Harvey Oswald as a communist."[41]

Garrison offers several pieces of evidence that link Oswald and Banister. When Banister died of an apparent heart attack in 1964, his widow Mary found a stack of handbills in his office identical to the ones Oswald had been handing out on the street in August 1963. Garrison believes these handbills, that said "Hands Off Cuba," and "Fair Play for Cuba," were provided by Banister and "left-overs from Lee Oswald's performances as [a Castro supporter]."[42]

These confusing incidents have left many wondering whether Oswald was really pro-Castro or an anti-Castro agent posing as a supporter of the Cuban dictator for an unknown CIA operation. The HSCA investigation into this question did little to throw light on the subject. According to their report, "The committee fully recognized that during the course of Oswald's activities in New Orleans he apparently became involved with certain anti-Castro elements, although such activities on Oswald's part have never been fully explained."[43]

A Fake Defector?

The mysteries surrounding these events have left some to conclude that Oswald was set up to look like a Communist so that people would believe that he had a reason to kill the president. While many think that Oswald never fired a shot and was a patsy made to look guilty, the Warren Report concludes:

More than One Oswald?

Many conspiracy researchers believe that someone set up Oswald to take the blame for the Kennedy assassination. Some even suppose that there were several people posing as Lee Harvey Oswald in order create negative attention toward the suspect.

In October 1963 U.S. security agents photographed a portly man leaving the Russian embassy in Mexico City. Although this man bore no resemblance to the suspect in Kennedy's murder, he was identified by the CIA as Lee Harvey Oswald.

Back in the United States, on November 9, 1963, just weeks before the assassination, a Dallas car salesman, Albert Bogard, met a man who identified himself as Lee Harvey Oswald. Bogard accompanied the man on a test-drive of a new car where the alleged Oswald went on a seventy-mile-per-hour, hair-raising drive through town, expertly handling the car around a series of sharp turns. He told the salesman that he would come back to buy the car because he was coming into a lot of money soon and, conversely, he was moving to Russia. The man arrested for killing Kennedy, however, did not know how to drive.

Around the same time, other witnesses recalled a man named Lee Oswald who was loud and obnoxious while buying ammunition at a gun shop. After making his purchase, the man drew further attention to himself at a nearby Dallas gun range. Instead of shooting at his own target, this Oswald angered other marksmen by shooting at their targets.

Whether or not the men seen at the gun range, car dealer, and embassy were impostors or the real Oswald remains unknown.

[long] before the assassination [Oswald] expressed his hatred for American society and acted in protest against it. . . . He sought for himself a place in history —a role as the "great man". . . . Out of these and the many other factors which may have molded the character of Lee Harvey Oswald, there emerged a man capable of assassinating President Kennedy.[44]

Many people remain skeptical about this assessment and Oswald's death just days after the assassination has insured that the world will never truly know the motives of Lee Harvey Oswald.

Chapter 4

Did the Mafia Kill Kennedy?

When John F. Kennedy was assassinated on November 22, 1963, millions of Americans expressed shock and confusion. Two days later, the case took a bizarre and unexpected twist when the president's accused assassin, Lee Harvey Oswald, was gunned down on live television by Jack Ruby. If Oswald knew who killed the president—or why—he took the secret to his grave.

With Oswald dead, attention turned to Jack Ruby, the eccentric owner of a seedy strip club in Dallas. In the following days, the press and the public began to ask questions: Who was Jack Ruby? What were his motives for the shooting? How did he elude stringent security in order to kill Oswald? Did Ruby's known ties to the Mafia have any connection to the Kennedy assassination? Similar questions had been asked about Oswald, and as with Oswald, the answers became less clear with time.

Ruby in the Shadows

When Jack Ruby leaped into the national spotlight it was quickly revealed that the nightclub owner had been seen at several key locations connected to the presidential assassination. Dallas newspaper reporter Seth Kantor met Ruby in the crowd at Parkland Memorial Hospital immediately after Kennedy was shot. Kantor and Ruby knew each other and exchanged a few words. Although Kantor told the Warren commissioners he saw Ruby at the hospital, the Warren Report says "Kantor may have been mistaken about both the time and the place that he saw Ruby."[45] The HSCA, however, believed Kantor's account and came to the opposite conclusion, saying that "While the Warren Commission concluded that Kantor was mistaken the [HSCA] committee determined he probably was not."[46] While no one knows why Ruby might have been at Parkland, Kantor believes the nightclub owner may have been planting the pristine "magic bullet" on Connally's stretcher in order to frame Oswald.

While Ruby's appearance at Parkland Memorial has been a matter of debate, photographs and films clearly show that the nightclub owner attended the Friday night press conference where Lee Harvey Oswald was questioned by reporters at the Dallas police station. During the news conference, Dallas district attorney Henry Wade named Oswald as a member of the "Free Cuba Committee." Ruby, standing at the back of the crowded room, corrected the district attorney, yelling out, "That's the Fair Play for Cuba Committee, Henry."[47] No one has been able to answer how or why Ruby had such intimate knowledge of Oswald's political activities.

It also remains a mystery as to how Ruby, two days later, managed to get through intense security in a heavily guarded basement of the Dallas police station in order to shoot Oswald. With more than seventy officers assembled, an armored truck in place to transfer the prisoner, and the basement cleared of all civilian personnel, some believe Ruby was purposely let in. The Warren Report speculates that Ruby walked past a single police officer who was guarding the ramp that led down into the basement parking lot. Others believe Ruby was let into the basement through a locked door by police officers who knew him as the owner of the Carousel Club.

Mafia Contacts

Ruby told authorities that he had killed Oswald so that Jacqueline Kennedy would not have to return to Dallas to

Virtually unnoticed, Jack Ruby approaches the prisoner with a gun. Moments later, he shoots Oswald.

testify at Oswald's trial. But Ruby was anything but an average citizen concerned for the well-being of the First Lady. In fact, at the time he shot Oswald, Ruby had been doing business with major Mafia leaders for more than thirty years.

Ruby was born on Chicago's crime-ridden West Side in 1911 and allegedly worked for the murderous gangster Al Capone in the 1930s. He later attempted to find a legal means of income by opening a string of nightclubs like the Carousel Club that he owned in Dallas. The club catered to members of the Texas underworld and also attracted a large number of Dallas policemen who enjoyed the free drinks Ruby provided for them. Ruby seemed to prefer police officers in his club because of the security their presence provided. As Dallas district attorney Bill Alexander says, having police at the Carousel was "better than having a bunch of hoodlums there. . . . Nobody was going to get rolled at his place with the type of police contacts he had there."[48]

While Ruby might have curried favor with the law, he also maintained close contacts with the Mafia. This came to light in 1967 when Jim Garrison investigated the Kennedy assassination. Garrison examined telephone

Jack Ruby stands outside his Carousel Club with two dancers. Ruby opened several nightclubs as a means of earning legitimate income.

records from the Carousel Club and Ruby's Dallas apartment in the months before Kennedy's murder and discovered that Ruby's phone calls to and from major Mafia figures increased twentyfold in the months before Kennedy's death. The calls began in late April when it was announced in newspapers that the president was going to visit Dallas in November. Some of these callers were mobsters whom Ruby had not seen in over twenty years. When the House Select Committee on Assassinations examined these phone records, it concluded that there was a possibility that the nightclub owner was part of a Mafia conspiracy to silence Oswald after the assassination. The HSCA report states:

> In assessing the significance of these Ruby contacts, the committee noted . . . [that] the pattern of contacts did show that individuals who had the motive to kill the President also had knowledge [that Ruby] could be used to get access to Oswald in the custody of the Dallas police. In Ruby, they also had knowledge of a man who had exhibited a violent nature and who was in serious financial trouble. The calls, in short, established knowledge and possible availability, if not actual planning.[49]

"The Most Bizarre Conspiracy"

Ruby's behavior became extremely erratic after he was arrested for shooting Oswald, and he feared that he himself might be the target of an assassin. When he was visited in jail by Earl Warren, Gerald Ford, and other members of the Warren Commission, Ruby was paranoid and nervous, shifting in his chair and compulsively chewing his lower lip. The commissioners dismissed Oswald's killer as mentally ill but Ruby begged the commissioners on eight occasions to take him to Washington, D.C., where he could speak without fear of retribution, saying "Gentlemen, unless you get

Chief Justice Warren leaves the Dallas County Jail after interrogating Jack Ruby.

me to Washington, you can't get a fair shake out of me. . . . My life is in danger here."[50] Although Warren could easily have ordered the transfer of Ruby to a secure facility in the capital, the killer's requests were refused.

After he was convicted of killing Oswald in March 1964, the jailed Ruby made many attention-grabbing claims. One was that Kennedy's death was the result of a conspiracy between wealthy Texas oilmen, Vice President Lyndon Johnson, and the Mafia. In 1967 Ruby told reporter Tom Johnson the Kennedy assassination "is the most bizarre conspiracy in the history of the world."[51]

Although he never named all of the individuals who might have conspired to kill Kennedy, Ruby claimed to have special knowledge in a 1967 interview:

> The only thing I can say is—everything pertaining to what's happened has never come to the surface. The world will never know the true facts of what

occurred—my motive, in other words. I am the only person in the background to know the truth pertaining to everything relating to my circumstances. . . . [The truth will never come out because] unfortunately these people, who have so much to gain and have such an ulterior motive to put me in the position I'm in, will never let the true facts come above-board [to be revealed] to the world.[52]

Ruby died of lung cancer in 1967 soon after he had been granted a new trial for Oswald's murder. As Richard Belzer writes: "He died protesting that the truth of the assassination was still not known."[53]

Was Ruby Sane?

Not everyone believed the ramblings of Ruby, however, and even his sister, Eva Grant, believed that he was insane. She told the Warren Commission that her brother "kept a picture of President Kennedy in his cell and kissed it during the day. He is mentally deranged."[54]

Yet Ruby's sanity and his questionable ramblings seemed to have been validated in the years after his death. In the 1970s Mafia boss Johnny Roselli told nationally syndicated newspaper columnist Jack Anderson: "When Oswald was [arrested], the underworld conspirators feared he would crack and disclose information that might lead to them. This most certainly would have brought a massive U.S. crackdown on the Mafia. So Jack Ruby was ordered to eliminate Oswald."[55] This statement led some to believe that Ruby might have been acting on Mafia orders, and that high-level mobsters were at the center of the Kennedy assassination.

In August 1976 Roselli himself died under mysterious circumstances; he was found shot to death, his dismembered body stuffed into an oil drum floating in the Atlantic Ocean near Miami. Some believe that his murder was retribution for speaking publicly about the Mafia's connection to Ruby.

"Assassinated as a Result of a Conspiracy"

The links between Ruby and the Mafia were never investigated by the Warren Commission which plainly states: "Ruby was not affiliated with organized criminal activity."[56] After Roselli made his comments, however, the final report by the House Select Committee on Assassinations connects the Mafia with the Kennedy assassination, saying: "President John F. Kennedy was probably assassinated as a result of a conspiracy. The committee is unable to identify the other gunman or the extent of the conspiracy." Despite this disclaimer, the report places several powerful Mafia leaders at the center of the plot, saying "the most likely family bosses of

Ensuring Mafia Silence

Sam Giancana and Johnny Roselli were ruthless Mafia bosses who ordered contract murders on hundreds of people including, some believe, President Kennedy. But conspiracy researchers say that even these men were not safe from those who wanted to keep the truth about the assassination from being discovered.

In 1975 a congressional investigative committee known as the Church Committee, because it was headed by Senator Frank Church, was organized to investigate CIA abuses, including the connections that the Agency had to Mafia hit men implicated in failed plots to kill Castro. These mobsters were also believed by some to be involved with the Kennedy assassination. Days before Giancana was scheduled to testify, he was found at home lying in a pool of blood. He had been shot once in the back of the head—and six times in a

neat circle around his mouth. Experts say this might have been a gruesome message to others who might talk to authorities about the secret assassination plots.

Further evidence is supplied by FBI surveillance tapes, quoted in *Conspiracy* by Anthony Summers. According to the tapes, after Giancana's death Trafficante said about himself and Carlos Marcello, "Now only two people are alive . . . who know who killed Kennedy. And [we] aren't talking."

In 1976 Roselli was another mobster called before the Church Committee. After testifying, he was seen dining with Trafficante. About two weeks later, Roselli was found strangled and stabbed, floating in the ocean in an oil drum near Miami. Before he died, Roselli informed the government that his Mafia partners in the Castro plots had gone on to kill Kennedy.

organized crime to [have] participated in such a unilateral assassination plan were Carlos Marcello and Santos Trafficante . . . [who both had] motive, means, and opportunity to have President John F. Kennedy assassinated."[57]

This finding generated dozens of books and articles linking Ruby, the Mafia, and the Kennedy assassination. Dallas reporter Seth Kantor wrote a book called *Who Was Jack Ruby?* that concluded that the nightclub owner was a Mafia hit man. In 1979 the *Washington Post* ran an in-depth article called "Did the Mafia Kill JFK?" And Robert Blakey, chief council to the HSCA wrote a book called *The Plot to Kill the President* that also concludes that the Mafia was involved with the assassination.

The HSCA report does not make the connection between the Mafia and the CIA in regard to Kennedy, but it does mention that the two organizations had worked together to assassinate Fidel Castro. And the report states that organized crime assisted the CIA because "a relationship with the CIA in the assassination of a foreign leader could be used by organized crime as leverage to prevent prosecution for unrelated offenses."[58] These facts support the conclusion of many who believe that when the Kennedy administration initiated criminal investigations into the activities of the Mafia, they betrayed this unspoken agreement and provided a motive for the Mafia to kill JFK.

The Mafia Vows Vengeance

Carlos Marcello, mentioned in the HSCA report, was a powerful and dangerous Mafia leader who controlled New Orleans. In the early sixties he was reputedly earning over $1.1 billion a year from various illegal activities, making his crime syndicate the largest business of any kind in Louisiana. This put him squarely in the sights of the Kennedy administration.

In 1961 when federal agents, on President Kennedy's orders, picked up Marcello and deported him to Guatemala, the mobster was humiliated and infuriated. After sneaking

Mobster Carlos Marcello commented in 1962 that he wanted Kennedy killed.

back into the country in September 1962 the angry Marcello held a meeting at his Churchill Farms estate outside New Orleans. According to a tape made by government agents who were investigating the mobster, Marcello made some threatening comments concerning the Kennedys at that meeting, saying that he wanted to see Kennedy killed. To hide his involvement, he said he would set it up so that some "nut" took the blame. Summers describes the event further:

> Marcello referred to President Kennedy as a dog, with his brother the Attorney General being the tail. He said, "The dog will keep biting you if you only cut off its tail," but that if the dog's head were cut off, the entire dog would die. The meaning of the analogy was clear—with John Kennedy dead, his younger brother would cease to be Attorney General, and the harassment of the Mafia would cease.[59]

About six months after Marcello made these comments, the mob boss was visited by Ruby, who was in New Orleans purportedly to hire strippers for his club. Upon returning to Dallas, Ruby began to keep company with Joseph Campisi, the number two man in the Dallas Mafia and a close friend of Marcello's. This later led to speculation that Campisi, on Marcello's orders, was briefing Ruby on his role in the assassination plot that was taking shape.

When the HSCA later examined the relationship between Campisi and Ruby they discovered that the two men had dined together on the night before Kennedy was assassinated. And, as Campisi testified before the House committee, he was the first person allowed to visit Ruby in the Dallas County jail eight days after the assassination. The purpose of this visit is spelled out in the HSCA report:

It is one of the practices of the Mafia to visit a member of the brotherhood who has been jailed for a crime in which the [Mafia] was involved soon after he first enters his cell. One of the purposes of such a visit is to remind the jailed colleague that he is to keep his mouth shut or else something unpleasant might happen to him or to a member of his family. This is usually done in subtle ways. . . .

The committee took note that Jack Ruby had dined with a Dallas-based member of the Marcello organization the evening before the assassination of the President and that the same Dallas-based member of the Marcello organization was the first person to visit Ruby after he had been jailed for the murder of the President's alleged assassin. The committee had little choice but to regard the Ruby-Campisi relationship

The Three Mysterious Tramps

Those who think that there was a plot to kill Kennedy believe that there were many conspirators in the crowd that day on Dealey Plaza. Most puzzling are the men called the three tramps who were arrested after the shooting. These men, taken into custody by police, were hiding in a boxcar that was about to pull out of the railroad yard behind Dealey Plaza. Although no record exists as to who these men were or why they were behind the grassy knoll, they were photographed by dozens of reporters at the time of their arrest. And despite the fact that the three men were dressed like hobos with dirty suits and pants, they had clean hands and new shoes. Some believe they were in disguise.

In the late 1970s conspiracy theorists charged that one of the three tramps was Charles B. Harrelson, a convicted hit man who was by then serving a life sentence for killing a federal judge in San Antonio. Harrelson has admitted to killing at least five other people, and is known to have worked for Santos Trafficante, Carlos Marcello, and others in the Dallas underworld; Jack Ruby is alleged to have said that Harrelson was his best friend. Although he denied he was one of the three tramps, the man in the photographs bears a striking resemblance to Harrelson.

The other two tramps are alleged to be E. Howard Hunt and Frank Sturgis. Both of these men took part in the burglary of the Democratic headquarters in the Watergate Office Complex in 1972, which resulted in the resignation of President Richard M. Nixon.

and the Campisi-Marcello relationship as yet another set of associations strengthening the committee's growing suspicion of the Marcello crime family's involvement in a conspiracy to assassinate President Kennedy or execute the President's alleged assassin or both.[60]

The Corsican Connection

Six years after the HSCA report tied the Mafia to Ruby, investigative journalist Stephen Rivele interviewed a man

Jack Ruby is led to jail after shooting Oswald. His first visitor in prison was a member of the Marcello crime organization.

who claimed to have firsthand knowledge of Marcello's direct involvement in the Kennedy assassination.

Rivele revealed that in 1984 he met several times with a French heroin smuggler named Christian David who was serving time in prison at Leavenworth, Kansas. David had been arrested while working for the branch of the Mafia based on the French island of Corsica. As a member of the Corsican mob, David was part of a well-known heroin-smuggling network of the 1970s called the "French Connection."

David told Rivele that he became aware of a conspiracy to murder Kennedy in May 1963, while in Marseille, France. At that time Antoine Guérini, a Corsican crime boss, allegedly offered David a contract to kill the president. David turned it down because he thought the job was too dangerous. Instead, David alleges that the contract was taken by three men—Lucien Sarti, also a Corsican drug trafficker and hit man, and two other members of the Marseille Mafia whose names David would not reveal for fear of reprisal. (Sarti died in 1972.) David claimed that he met Sarti and the two others in Buenos Aires, Argentina, several years after the assassination and they told him how the assassination was carried out. David's story is printed on "The French Connection," a website that deals with the alleged Mafia conspiracy to kill the president:

About two weeks before the assassination, Sarti flew from France to Mexico City, from where he drove . . . to a private house in Dallas. . . . David said [Sarti and the other] assassins cased Dealey Plaza, took photographs and worked out mathematically how to set up a crossfire [in order to kill Kennedy]. Sarti wanted to fire from the triple underpass bridge, but when he arrived in Dealey Plaza the day of the assassination, there were people there, so he fired from a little hill next to the bridge. There was a wooden fence on that hill, and Sarti fired from behind the wooden fence. He said Sarti only fired once, and used an explosive bullet. [David] said Kennedy was shot in a crossfire, two shots from behind, and Sarti's shot from the front. . . . The first shot was fired from behind and hit Kennedy in the back. The second shot was fired from behind, and hit "the other person in the car [Connally]." The third shot was fired from in front, and hit Kennedy in the head. The fourth shot was from behind and missed "because the car was too far away." He said that two shots were almost simultaneous.[61]

David went on to claim that Sarti wore a police officer's uniform for disguise. After the assassination, Sarti and the other assassins hid in Dallas for several weeks and then traveled to Montreal, Canada, where they took a flight back to Marseille.

Sarti told David that Kennedy was killed out of revenge for his administration's crackdown on the Mafia. Sarti also said that some members of the CIA who had worked with the Mafia to assassinate Castro had prior knowledge of the plot and let it proceed out of hatred for Kennedy. As Sarti said, the "CIA was incapable of killing Kennedy but . . . they did cover it up."[62]

Confirming the Story

Since David was a known drug trafficker and heroin addict and had little credibility, Rivele tried to verify his story by seeking out another man, Michel Nicoli, who David said had also heard Sarti discuss the assassination in Buenos Aires. Nicoli was a former drug trafficker turned government informant who had testified against French Connection members in 1972. He was living under the U.S. government's witness protection program that hides informants from retaliation against criminals who are jailed because of informant testimony. After a long search traveling thousands of miles

Advanced Knowledge of the Plot

The Mafia and anti-Castro groups had connections to right-wing extremists, such as Joseph Milteer, who have also been linked to the Kennedy assassination. Milteer was a white supremacist and political activist from Quitman, Georgia. On a trip to Miami, thirteen days before Kennedy was killed, Milteer had a conversation with government informant William Somersett that was secretly taped by police investigators. On the tape Milteer seems to be discussing in accurate detail how the president would be murdered less than two weeks later. The following transcript of that conversation was published in *Conspiracy* by Anthony Summers:

> [Somersett]: I think Kennedy is coming here on the 18th, or something like that to make some kind of speech. . . .
>
> [Milteer]: You can bet your bottom dollar he is going to have a lot to say about the Cubans. There are so many of them here.
>
> [Somersett]: Yeah. Well, he will have a thousand bodyguards, don't worry about that.

> [Milteer]: The more bodyguards he has the easier it is to get him.
>
> [Somersett]: Well, how in the hell do you figure would be the best way to get him?
>
> [Milteer]: From an office building with a high-powered rifle. . . . He knows he's a marked man. . . .
>
> [Somersett]: They are really going to try to kill him?
>
> [Milteer]: Oh yeah, it is in the working . . . .
>
> [Somersett]: Boy, if that Kennedy gets shot, we have to know where we are at. Because you know that will be a real shake if they do that.
>
> [Milteer]: They wouldn't leave any stone unturned there, no way. They will pick somebody up within hours afterwards, if anything like that would happen. Just to throw the public off.

throughout North and South America, Rivele found Nicoli with the help of a high-level official in the U.S. Drug Enforcement Administration (DEA). Rivele claims that the DEA official said that Nicoli was the most trustworthy witness he ever had in thirty years in the business, and if he told you something "you could take it to the bank."[63]

According to Rivele, Nicoli confirmed David's story and also said the assassins had been paid with a large quantity of heroin which Nicoli himself had converted into cash for them. From further interviews Rivele deduced who initiated the plot: "My own conviction at this point is that the contract probably originated with Carlos Marcello of New Orleans who placed it in Marseilles through his colleague Santo

Trafficante, Jr."[64] Nicoli said the Mafia bosses hired highly experienced, foreign assassins without direct ties to the American Mafia in order "to obliterate any traces; to fool the government. It's more difficult to find foreign killers."[65]

Rivele was risking his life by talking about this alleged plot. Despite death threats in both France and the United States, Rivele continued to pursue his leads. In 1987 Rivele turned over his information to the FBI. A federal agent spoke with Nicoli and was convinced that his story was accurate. But the agents told Rivele that it was standard procedure to produce at least two corroborating witnesses in order to convince a grand jury to arrest the alleged plotters. David refused to testify, and Rivele had no other witnesses, so nothing ever came of the investigation. In 2001 Rivele commented on the alleged plot that killed Kennedy:

> I have not touched the case since 1988 . . . it eats your soul. David was released from prison a few years ago and is alive in France. I assume that Nicoli is still alive. . . . I saw a documentary TV show last year about the [Soviet secret service organization] KGB's investigation of the assassination, and was amazed to learn that they came to the same conclusion as me. Second, I was contacted two years ago by a former CIA agent . . . who told me that I was right about the assassination. Small comfort but better than nothing.[66]

"He Is Going to Be Hit"

Although Rivele gave up his quest for answers, several of Trafficante's associates have linked the Mafia boss to the Kennedy assassination. In 1976 wealthy Cuban exile José Aleman told a *Washington Post* reporter of a conversation he had with Trafficante in 1962. At that time Trafficante, complaining about the government's investigation into Mafia activities, told Aleman: "Mark my words, this man Kennedy is in trouble, and he will get what is coming to him." Aleman argued that Kennedy would easily win reelection in 1964, but Trafficante said, "No, José, he is going to be hit."[67]

After this comment was made public, Trafficante was called before the House Select Committee on Assassinations. The mob boss was asked if he ever plotted to assassinate Kennedy, if he knew Jack Ruby prior to November 22, 1963, and if he was ever visited by Ruby when he was in Cuba. To all three questions, Trafficante refused to answer, "pleading the fifth," that is stating that the Fifth Amendment of the Constitution guarantees no person shall be compelled in any criminal case to be a witness against himself. When Trafficante lay dying in 1987, however, his longtime attorney Frank Ragano claims that the Mafia boss expressed remorse over Kennedy's murder while blaming Carlos Marcello. Ragano claims that Trafficante said: "Carlo [screwed] up. We should not have killed [John]. We should have killed Bobby."[68]

Santo Trafficante Jr. waves off reporters. The Mafia boss reportedly claimed that Kennedy was to be "hit."

Trafficante's alleged confession and the conclusions of the HSCA report have led many to believe that the Mafia did indeed order the assassination of JFK—and this was immediately apparent to top-level officials within the CIA, FBI, and the White House. With the top-secret knowledge that various government agents were actively working with the Mafia in plots against Castro, a disclosure implicating the Mafia might have embarrassed the CIA and even led to a war with Cuba's benefactor, the Soviet Union. Whether or not this is true, it adds an intriguing element to the Kennedy murder mystery and brings up many questions that will probably never be answered.

Chapter 5

Was the Government Involved?

M ore than forty years after the fact, the assassination of President Kennedy still seems an audacious act. How and why this was accomplished remains the subject of much speculation. Many theories presented over the years allege that members of the CIA, FBI, Defense Department, or even elected officials might have orchestrated the assassination or at least participated in a cover-up.

While none of these shocking theories has been proven, questions about the government's role in Kennedy's death have filtered into the general population. According to a 1998 poll conducted by CBS News, more than three out of four Americans—77 percent—believe there were conspirators such as government agents involved in the Kennedy assassination. The same poll showed that 68 percent think there was an official government cover-up to keep the public from learning the truth. And people remain skeptical that the truth will ever be known, with 84 percent agreeing that the government will never tell the public what really happened.

One area of speculation about government involvement concerns the sequence of events after the president was pronounced dead. In particular, questions have been raised

Jacqueline Kennedy, daughter Caroline (foreground), and members of the Kennedy family stand in the Capitol Rotunda during a memorial service for the slain president.

about who was in charge of Kennedy's autopsy, why it was conducted in the manner it was, and whether vital evidence was altered or stolen after the president was buried.

Did Someone Tamper with the Body?

Immediately after his death, as Kennedy lay dead on a stretcher at Parkland Memorial Hospital, Secret Service agents angrily tried to prevent Dallas County medical examiner Earl Rose from performing an autopsy on the president. While Jacqueline Kennedy stood watching, an argument ensued between Rose and government agents, with heavily armed agents cursing loudly and threatening the doctor with physical harm. Finally, over the angry protests of Dallas County officials, the casket was wheeled out of the hospital. But as Douglas Weldon writes in James H. Fetzer's *Murder in Dealey Plaza* the Secret Service was acting illegally when agents forcibly removed Kennedy's body from the hospital:

> It is critical to understand that in 1963 there was no federal statute that made it a crime to kill the President of the United States. Legally, this was simply a murder that should have been governed by the statutes of the state of Texas. Texas had the sole authority to investigate the crime, to take evidence into its custody, to perform the autopsy on the deceased president, and to pursue any criminal prosecution that might result therefrom.[69]

Confusion over who should have control of the body might have been understandable under the circumstances. Local and federal agents had no experience with a presidential assassination, after all. But the failure to perform an impartial autopsy immediately after the killing made it impossible to determine how many bullets hit the president and from what angle. As forensic coroner Charles G. Wilber writes in *Medicolegal Investigation of the President John F. Kennedy Murder:*

> When the president was finally pronounced legally dead, there should have been a complete external examination of the entire body to catalog *all* the wounds visible and to describe them anatomically. [Instead Kennedy was] completely disrobed and wrapped in sheets for transportation in a casket. . . .
>
> There is every reason to contend that had the Secret Service and other federal agents not flouted Texas law . . . a proper . . . examination would have been made and in all probability the deluge of unbelief would have been prevented.[70]

Autopsy Oddities

After taking control at Parkland Memorial, agents placed the president's body in a top-of-the-line, ornate bronze casket which was taken to Love Field and jostled up the steps onto *Air Force One*. Upon arrival in Washington, D.C., the president's remains were transported by helicopter to the nearby Naval Medical Center at Bethesda, Maryland.

When the body was wheeled into the autopsy room at the naval hospital, medical technician Paul O'Connor noticed that it was in a cheap, plain, $150 shipping casket totally unlike the $4,000 casket witnesses had seen in Dallas. And, according to O'Connor, somewhere between Dallas and Bethesda, Kennedy's body had been transferred to a slate-gray, zippered rubber body bag, the type used by the military in combat situations. The sheet that had been wrapped around the president's body in Dallas was now only around his face and head. Since the First Lady remained near her husband's coffin the entire flight to Washington, it remains a mystery how this might have happened. Some have suggested that the president's body was tampered with in the helicopter ride to Bethesda.

Strange events continued to unfold as the president's body was rolled into the autopsy room at Bethesda at 8 P.M. Under almost any circumstances in which a murder is committed, authorities bring in doctors called forensic pathologists who are experts not only in medicine but also issues of law. These specialists are trained to discover important details about injuries that result in death. According to Wilber, at the time of the Kennedy assassination, the nation's leading forensic pathologists and gunshot wound experts all lived within a sixty-minute flight of Bethesda. These men, however, were not called upon to perform what has been widely referred to as the "autopsy of the century." Instead, two career military doctors, James J. Humes and J. Thornton Boswell, were ordered by the surgeon general of the navy to scrutinize Kennedy's remains.

Inexplicably, Humes and Boswell, administrators at the Naval Medical Center, had, between them, examined only a single case of a gunshot wound before the Kennedy autopsy. As Gerald Posner writes: "Hospital pathologists such as Humes and Boswell are not trained in the forensic aspects of autopsies or the search for clues in unnatural deaths, nor do they normally preserve evidence for subsequent medical or legal proceedings."[71]

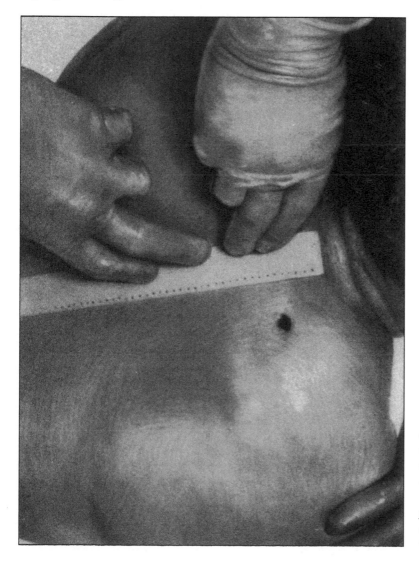

A drawing shows an examiner measuring one of the wounds on the president's back. The pathologists who performed the autopsy had scant experience with gunshot wounds.

As the two doctors prepared for the autopsy, the room filled with thirty-three nonmedical personnel including admirals, generals, and agents of the FBI, CIA, and Secret Service. Because so many witnesses could distract doctors during delicate procedures, Wilber believes that their presence was "quite contrary to medical directives and good autopsy practice."[72]

These men were anything but solemn witnesses to the presidential autopsy. Several of those in attendance, described by O'Connor as sinister-looking men in civilian clothes, took control of the situation. They told the doctors which procedures to perform—and which procedures not to perform. For example, one doctor testified that when he moved to dissect the wound in the back-throat region, he was ordered to stop. Without such a dissection, it is impossible to know for certain whether Kennedy was shot from the front or the back.

Such interference in an autopsy violated the *Autopsy Manual* issued by the Armed Forces Institute of Pathology that is the basis for all military personnel, such as Humes and Boswell, who perform autopsies. Nor did the Kennedy autopsy meet civilian standards. As autopsy expert and Warren Commission critic Cyril Wecht states, Kennedy's autopsy was

> extremely superficial and sloppy, inept, incomplete, incompetent in many respects, not only on the part of the pathologists who did this horribly inadequate medical-legal autopsy but on the part of many other people. This is the kind of examination that would not be tolerated in a routine murder case by a good crew of homicide detectives in most major cities of America on anybody, just a plain ordinary citizen, let alone a President.[73]

While no one has been able to explain why the autopsy of a murdered president was conducted in this manner, Wilber writes that it

Medical Contradictions

In *Medicolegal Investigation of the President John F. Kennedy Murder*, forensic coroner Charles G. Wilber describes some of the many discrepancies concerning the medical evidence in President Kennedy's murder:

> Interpretation of the fatal head wound by several attending surgeons [at Parkland Memorial Hospital] suggested a high-velocity handgun bullet fired at close range.
>
> Attending surgeons who rendered aid to the moribund President observed and described a gunshot wound in the left temple. This wound was later ignored by the investigating [Warren] Commission.
>
> The dead President's remains were spirited away illegally out of the jurisdiction of the Dallas coroner by the use of force, violence, and subterfuge on the part of federal officials. Texas law prohibits removal of a body from the state without an autopsy. . . .
>
> An inadequate autopsy was performed on the President's remains at Bethesda Naval Hospital. Critical . . . directions spelled out in the official Armed Forces Institute of Pathology *Autopsy Manual* were flagrantly ignored by the military autopsy pathologists, probably under orders from superior officers.
>
> A mysterious ["magic"] bullet of unverified origin and in questionable condition was used by the Warren Commission as serious and indeed key evidence.
>
> The head wounds as described by the pathologists at Bethesda seemed to be different than the head wound described by the attending surgeons [at Parkland].
>
> Odd pieces of skull, presumably from the President's head, were brought to the pathologists by Secret Service Agents when the autopsy was nearly over. Other fragments appeared and disappeared during the days after the autopsy. . . .
>
> Most, if not all, of the photographs said to have been taken at the autopsy are unverified and may have no . . . value.

is clear that those in charge were not going to permit the "whole truth" to come out. In this peculiar situation one must include the highest ranks of the Department of Defense, notably the Navy, the Secret Service, the FBI, and mysterious generals in and out of uniform whose names are now forgotten but who seemed to have been giving orders that night.[74]

To insure secrecy all military personnel working in the autopsy room that night were ordered to sign an official document threatening arrest which stated: "You are reminded that you are under verbal orders . . . to discuss with no one events concerning your official duties [at the autopsy]. . . . You are warned that infraction of these orders makes you liable to Court Martial proceedings."[75]

Forged Photos?

While eyewitnesses to the autopsy were silenced by military order, the official photographs taken during the autopsy would have been able to speak volumes about the nature of the president's wounds. But according to Wilber these unimpeachable records were "spirited away by presumed Secret Service agents and hidden somewhere. A roll of film exposed by a Navy enlisted technician was destroyed by some government 'agent.'"[76] Why these photos were suppressed is a matter of conjecture but some believe that they showed evidence that Kennedy was shot from the front and the back, therefore proving the existence of two shooters.

Meanwhile another set of photos said to be taken at the president's autopsy are believed by some to be forgeries. When a bullet enters a body, it makes a smaller hole upon entry and leaves a large exit wound as it continues on its trajectory. Forty expert witnesses in Dallas, including Kennedy's personal physician, stated that Kennedy had a small entrance wound on the side of his skull and a gaping exit wound in the back of his head meaning his fatal head shot came from in front of the limousine. However, when the autopsy photos that might have showed this were released in the mid-1970s, they revealed only a small, neat entrance wound at the front of the president's head. These images were not anything like the actual wound according to Dr. Gary Aguilar who writes:

> FBI agents who saw the autopsy images of JFK's skull wound testified under oath . . . that JFK's fatal skull wound looked nothing at all like the photographs that showed the backside of JFK's skull and scalp intact. . . . Either 40+ witnesses . . . were

wrong about JFK's rearward skull injury, or JFK's autopsy photographs were falsified in some manner to mask the rearward skull damage that these credible witnesses described.[77]

How the photos were doctored—if they were doctored—is a matter of debate. Some forensic experts who have studied them believe that Kennedy's scalp and hair were pulled over the exit wound when the photos were taken. Others think

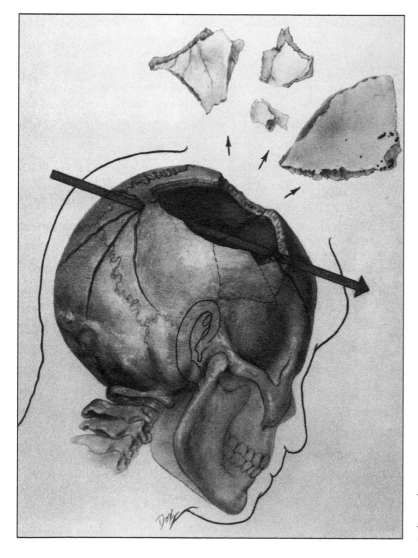

The Warren Commission published this picture to show the path Oswald's bullet might have taken as it passed through Kennedy's skull.

the photographs were altered using a technique called "soft edge matte insertion" in which a piece of another picture was pasted into the autopsy photos. Conspiracy researchers believe this could only have taken place with high-level cooperation.

The discrepancy between the photos and the president's wounds might explain why the Warren Commission refused to even study the pictures. If they had done so, they would have had to publish them in the Warren Report where they would have been seen by millions of people. Instead the commissioners studied drawings made after the autopsy. As Wilber writes:

> Instead of presenting photographs made at the autopsy and x-rays also taken during the course of the autopsy, a procedure that would have been routine in any other kind of investigation, an enlisted medical corps sailor was assigned to produce what were called . . . "schematic drawings." These schematics were based on oral instructions from Commander Humes and several of his associates.

The Strange Death of William Pitzer

Conspiracy researchers charge that another mysterious witness death is associated with Kennedy's autopsy photos. Navy lieutenant commander William Pitzer took the original photos of Kennedy at Bethesda Naval Hospital. Afterward, government officials subjected him to hour after hour of interrogation during which time he says officials ordered him to say the huge exit wound he had seen and photographed was really an entrance wound. Pitzer refused to change his story, however, and was supposedly working on a film about the autopsy in 1965

when he was found in his office at the hospital, dead from a gunshot wound to the right temple. His death was ruled a suicide, but many people, including his family, question that conclusion. They refused to believe that this tough military man would commit suicide. In addition, Pitzer was shot in the right temple, which investigators thought was odd since he was left-handed.

These incidents lead conspiracy researchers to conclude that the lieutenant commander was killed because he was about to go public with information about Kennedy's autopsy cover-up.

Oral descriptions only were available to the sailor who was supposed to draw a meaningful sketch of the wounds including size, location, and the like. . . .

Any ordinary citizen in his right mind would have known that a photograph of a wound is essential to give precise location, shape, etc. No artist's drawing, no matter how precise and exact, can reflect the nature of a wound.[78]

Critics of the conspiracy theories point to reasons why they believe Kennedy's autopsy photos were never published. As Gerald Posner writes: "Robert Kennedy, who feared the public display of the X-rays and photos would be offensive to the Kennedy family, reached an agreement with the Warren Commission not to publish the materials."[79]

Were There Two Brains?

Perhaps the most macabre aspect of the autopsy controversy concerns the president's brain. In Dallas doctors reported 20 to 25 percent of Kennedy's brain was missing as a result of the head shot while 75 percent remained intact in his skull. By the time Kennedy's remains reached Bethesda, however, the portion of the president's brain affected by the gunshot had disappeared and less than 50 percent of the remaining brain was found by doctors.

In most murder investigations involving a gunshot wound, the brain is removed and sectioned into quarters to trace the trajectory of the bullet. This allows forensic pathologists to determine the angle from which the bullet entered the skull. In addition bullet fragments, which contain unique microscopic markings, are retrieved in order to link them to the rifle from which they were fired. None of this could be accomplished in the Kennedy case, however, because the critical portion of the president's brain had mysteriously disappeared.

The intact portion of the president's brain was photographed by navy photographer John T. Stringer at an examination on the morning of November 25. Kennedy was buried—with his brain, according to his family—later that day. A doctor at Bethesda, however, said that he was asked by Humes to examine Kennedy's brain four days later on November 29. Yet another doctor said he examined what was said to be Kennedy's brain on December 2. These brains, however, may not even have belonged to the president.

In 1998 photos found in the National Archives were said to show the steps taken during Kennedy's brain autopsy. These pictures, however, show wounds that were markedly different from the wounds sustained by the president. According to an article in the *Washington Post* by George Lardner Jr.:

> Doctors who conducted the autopsy on President John F. Kennedy may have performed two brain examinations in the days following his assassination, possibly of two different brains. . . . [Brain] photographs in the Kennedy records are not of Kennedy's brain and show much less damage than Kennedy sustained when he was shot in Dallas. . . .
>
> Stringer said the photos he took . . . did not resemble those at the Archives. He said they seemed to be on "a different type of film" from the one he used. He said he also took photographs of "cross sections of the brain" that had been cut out. . . . No such photos are in the Archives collection.[80]

If these allegations are true, unknown government officials might have substituted a damaged brain from an unknown person for that of President Kennedy. The significance of this is explained by Douglas Horne, the chief analyst for Kennedy's assassination records at the National Archives: "I am 90 to 95 percent certain that the photographs in the Archives are not of President Kennedy's brain. . . . If they aren't, that can mean only one thing—that there has been a coverup of the medical evidence."[81]

Tampering with Photographs?

Over the years, researchers, congressional committees, and medical and photographic experts have studied the matter of President Kennedy's autopsy photos. These experts have found that photos thought to exist have disappeared while others have been tampered with. Their findings are summarized by Gary Aguilar in *Murder in Dealey Plaza:*

> All three of JFK's [doctors] . . . and both autopsy photographers recalled that specific photographs were taken during the President's autopsy that do not now exist.
>
> Chief White House photographer, Robert Knudsen told the [House Select Committee on Assassinations] . . . that right after the assassination he developed images that do not now exist.
>
> In 1997 former government photographer Joe O'Donnell [said] that in 1963 his friend, Robert Knudsen, showed him a photograph of JFK's head that revealed a large hole in the backside of the skull. No such image can now be found in the official inventory.

Naval Photographic Center employee Saundra Spencer [said] that while developing JFK's autopsy photographs shortly after the assassination she, like Joseph O'Donnell, also saw an image revealing a hole in the back of JFK's skull. She also claimed that the film on which current autopsy photographs appear is film that was not used in the lab that is supposed to have developed the films in 1963.

Chief autopsy photographer John Stringer disavowed the . . . autopsy photographs of JFK's brain. Though Stringer was the photographer of record, he swore . . . that he did not take the extant images. Moreover, he said that the current images were taken on film he is certain he did not use. . . .

Upon being shown the autopsy photographs for the first time in 1997, the two FBI agents who witnessed the autopsy, Francis X. O'Neill and James Sibert, [said] the image showing the backside of JFK's skull intact had been, as agent O'Neill put it, "doctored." Both agents claimed there was a sizable defect in the rear of JFK's skull.

The Mystery Continues

The allegations about forged and destroyed evidence have led many to wonder who in the government could have been involved and why. No one has ever proven that there was a government conspiracy to kill Kennedy or cover up the evidence.

With each passing year it becomes less likely that the truth will ever be known about the Kennedy assassination. Many of those closest to the case have died and the memories of witnesses grow dim. But discoveries such as the mysterious brain photos in the National Archives continue to stir debate.

When President Kennedy was shot on November 22, 1963, an unnamed editor of the *New York Times* said: "The year 2000 will see men still arguing and writing about the President's death."[82] Although 2000 has come and gone, the editor's words still ring true in the twenty-first century.

People disagree as to why the assassination remains such an emotional topic four decades after the event. But many speak of Kennedy's presidency as a time of innocence, trust, and hope. In the years that followed the Kennedy assassination, millions of Americans lost faith in

President John F. Kennedy's body lies in state in the Capitol Rotunda. Controversy continues to surround his assassination.

their government when they discovered that important issues concerning the Vietnam War had been misrepresented by officials. The 1973 resignation of President Richard M. Nixon over the Watergate burglary and the 1976 revelations about CIA involvement with the Mafia only served to harden these feelings of distrust in the public mind. As respected English philosopher and statesman Bertrand Russell said in 1964: "There has never been a more subversive, conspiratorial, unpatriotic, or endangering course for the United States and the world than the attempt by the United States to hide the truth behind the murder of its recent president." [83]

Despite Russell's words, people continue to hope for the truth so that the national nightmare that came to pass on the streets of Dallas in November 1963 can finally be put to rest. Whether or not the facts will ever be known is a question that no one can answer.

Notes

Introduction: Who Killed JFK?

1. Quoted in Craig Frizzell and Magen Knuth, "Did President Kennedy Plan on Splintering the CIA?" JFK and the CIA: Mortal Enemies? http://mcadams.posc. mu.edu/jfk_cia.htm.

Chapter 1: Death in Dallas

2. Quoted in Robert J. Groden, *The Killing of a President: The Complete Photographic Record of the JFK Assassination, the Conspiracy and the Cover-Up*. New York: Viking Studio, 1993, p. 9.
3. Quoted in *Kennedy Assassination Home Page*, "Findings of the Select Committee on Assassinations in the Assassination of President John F. Kennedy in Dallas, Tex., November 22, 1963." http://jfkassassination. net/russ/jfkinfo/hscareport.htm.
4. Quoted in *Kennedy Assassination Home Page*, "Findings of the Select Committee on Assassinations."
5. Quoted in Anthony Summers, *Conspiracy*. New York: Paragon House, 1989, p. 3.
6. Summers, *Conspiracy*, p. 3.
7. Quoted in Groden, *The Killing of a President*, p. 101.
8. Quoted in Summers, *Conspiracy*, p. 55.
9. Quoted in Summers, *Conspiracy*, p. 107.
10. Quoted in Richard Belzer, *UFOs, JFK, and Elvis*. New York: Ballantine, 1999, p. 29.

11. *Report of the Warren Commission on the Assassination of President Kennedy*. New York: McGraw-Hill, 1964, pp. 41–42.
12. Quoted in *Report of the Warren Commission*, pp. xv–xvi.
13. Quoted in Summers, *Conspiracy*, p. 493.
14. Gerald Posner, *Case Closed: Lee Harvey Oswald and the Assassination of JFK*. New York: Random House, 1993, pp. ix–x.

Chapter 2: How Many Bullets Were Fired?

15. *Report of the Warren Commission*, p. 107.
16. *Report of the Warren Commission*, p. 107.
17. Mark Lane, *Rush to Judgment*. New York: Thunder's Mouth, 1992, p. 69.
18. Quoted in "Governor Connally's Wrist Wound and CE-399," Warren Commission Exhibit CE-399—The Magic Bullet. www.jfk-info.com/ fragment.htm.
19. *Kennedy Assassination Home Page*, "Findings of the Select Committee on Assassinations."
20. Quoted in Belzer, *UFOs, JFK, and Elvis*, p. 15.
21. *Report of the Warren Commission*, p. 102.
22. *Report of the Warren Commission*, p. 100.
23. *Kennedy Assassination Home Page*, "Findings of the Select Committee on Assassinations.

24. Quoted in James H. Fetzer, ed., *Murder in Dealey Plaza*. Chicago: Catfeet, 2000, p. 184.

25. Belzer, *UFOs, JFK, and Elvis*, pp. 46–47.

26. Quoted in Belzer, *UFOs, JFK, and Elvis*, p. 42.

27. Posner, *Case Closed*, p. 257.

28. Posner, *Case Closed*, p. 253.

Chapter 3: Who Was Oswald and Did He Kill the President?

29. Quoted in Mae Brussell, "The Last Words of Lee Harvey Oswald." http://www.ratical.org/ratville/JFK/LHO.html, May 28, 1992.

30. Quoted in Posner, *Case Closed*, p. 225.

31. Quoted in *Report of the Warren Commission*, p. 132.

32. Quoted in Brussell, "The Last Words of Lee Harvey Oswald."

33. Quoted in Brussell, "The Last Words of Lee Harvey Oswald."

34. *Report of the Warren Commission*, p. 117.

35. Quoted in Salvador Astucia, "Chapter Six: Other Garrison Findings," *Opium Lords*, April 2002. www.jfkmontreal.com/other_garrison.htm.

36. Jim Garrison, *On the Trail of the Assassins*. New York: Warner, 1988, pp. 58–59.

37. Quoted in Garrison, *On the Trail of the Assassins*, p. 59.

38. Quoted in Posner, *Case Closed*, p. 107.

39. Quoted in Posner, *Case Closed*, p. 114.

40. *Report of the Warren Commission*, p. 406.

41. Garrison, *On the Trail of the Assassins*, p. 29.

42. Garrison, *On the Trail of the Assassins*, p. 41.

43. *Kennedy Assassination Home Page*, "Findings of the Select Committee on Assassinations."

44. *Report of the Warren Commission*, p. 399.

Chapter 4: Did the Mafia Kill Kennedy?

45. *Report of the Warren Commission*, p. 315.

46. *Kennedy Assassination Home Page*, "Findings of the Select Committee on Assassinations."

47. Quoted in Dave Reitzes, "Oswald and Ruby," LHO and Ruby. www.acorn.net/jfkplace/03/JA/DR/.dr06.html.

48. Quoted in Posner, *Case Closed*, p. 359.

49. *Kennedy Assassination Home Page*, "Findings of the Select Committee on Assassinations."

50. Quoted in Groden, *The Killing of a President*, p. 110.

51. Quoted in Groden, *The Killing of a President*, p. 110.

52. Quoted in Summers, *Conspiracy*, p. 472.

53. Belzer, *UFOs, JFK, and Elvis*, p. 100.

54. Quoted in Gerald Posner, *Case Closed*, p. 401.

55. Quoted in Summers, *Conspiracy*, p. 471.

56. Report of the Warren Commission, p. 707.

57. *Kennedy Assassination Home Page*, "Findings of the Select Committee on Assassinations."

58. *Kennedy Assassination Home Page*, "Findings of the Select Committee on Assassinations."

59. Summers, *Conspiracy*, p. 258.

60. *House Select Committee on Assassinations*, "The HSCA on Jack Ruby's Mafia Links."

http://ourworld-top.cs.com/mikegriffith1/id153.htm.

61. Noel Twyman, "The French Connection," *Doug's JFK Assassination Page*. http://www.geocities.com/metsman_2001/french.html.

62. Quoted in Noel Twyman, *Bloody Treason*. Rancho Santa Fe, CA: Laurel, 1977, p. 418.

63. Quoted in Twyman, "The French Connection."

64. Quoted in "Introduction," The Corsican Connection. http://members.optushome.com.au/tnorth/introduction.htm.

65. Quoted in "Introduction," The Corsican Connection.

66. Quoted in "Introduction," The Corsican Connection.

67. Quoted in Ronald L. Ecker, "Hell in Miami," *Hodge & Braddock*, May 17, 2002. www.hobrad.com/acrehell.htm.

68. Quoted in Ecker, "Hell in Miami."

Chapter 5: Was the Government Involved?

69. Quoted in Fetzer, *Murder in Dealey Plaza*, p. 132.

70. Charles G. Wilber, *Medicolegal Investigation of the President John F. Kennedy Murder*. Springfield, IL: Charles C. Thomas, 1978, pp. 94–95.

71. Posner, *Case Closed*, p. 300.

72. Wilber, *Medicolegal Investigation*, p. 96.

73. Dr. Cyril Wecht, Testimony Before House Select Committee on Assassinations. www.jmasland.com/testimony/hsca_med/wecht.htm.

74. Wilber, *Medicolegal Investigation*, p. 102.

75. Quoted in David S. Lifton, *Best Evidence*. New York: Macmillan, 1980, p. 607.

76. Wilber, *Medicolegal Investigation*, p. 103.

77. Quoted in Fetzer, *Murder in Dealey Plaza*, p. 189.

78. Wilber, *Medicolegal Investigation*, pp. 6–7.

79. Posner, *Case Closed*, p. 307.

80. George Lardner Jr., "Archive Photos Not of JFK's Brain, Concludes Aide to Review Board Staff Member," *Washington Post*, November 10, 1998. www.jaxinter.net/~cheryl/news.html.

81. Quoted in Lardner, "Archive Photos Not of JFK's Brain."

82. Quoted in *Report of the Warren Commission*, p. xvi.

83. Quoted in Belzer, *UFOs, JFK, and Elvis*, p. 35.

For Further Reading

Books

Bob Callahan, *Who Shot JFK? A Guide to the Major Conspiracy Theories.* New York: Fireside, 1993. A guide to the major conspiracy theories concerning Kennedy's assassination with sections and sidebars on Jack Ruby, Lee Harvey Oswald, and dozens of other alleged players in the plot.

Michael Canfield and Alan J. Weberman, *Coup d'État in America: The CIA and the Assassination of John F. Kennedy.* New Rochelle, NY: Third Press, 1992. A book that ties together the various alleged entities in the Kennedy assassination into a single theory that has been embraced by many conspiracy researchers.

Wilborn Hampton, *Kennedy Assassinated! The World Mourns: A Reporter's Story.* Cambridge, MA: Candlewick, 1997. A minute-by-minute chronicle of what happened the day Kennedy was shot. Historic news photographs appear on almost every page.

Clarice Swisher, ed., *People Who Made History: John F. Kennedy.* San Diego: Greenhaven, 1999. This anthology profiles Kennedy's unique style and personality and describes his domestic and foreign policy successes and failures.

Michael V. Uschan, *John F. Kennedy.* San Diego: Lucent, 1999. A biography of the thirty-fifth president of the United States who served from 1961 until his assassination in 1963.

Internet Source

Christopher Mann, "Dealey Plaza, Kennedy Assassination Site," *Virtual Visitor.* http://search.yahoo.com/bin/search?p=dealey+plaza. A Quicktime Panoramic Movie of Dealey Plaza where visitors can use their mouse and keyboard controls to view the entire site where Kennedy was assassinated.

Works Consulted

Books

Richard Belzer, *UFOs, JFK, and Elvis*. New York: Ballantine, 1999. Actor, comedian, and conspiracy theorist Belzer combines humor, facts, and speculation to discuss various historic cover-ups, plots, and schemes.

James H. Fetzer, ed., *Murder in Dealey Plaza*. Chicago: Catfeet, 2000. A collection of articles exploring different technological and scientific aspects of the Kennedy assassination.

Jim Garrison, *On the Trail of the Assassins*. New York: Warner, 1988. Written by the former district attorney of New Orleans, this book is a record of the evidence that prompted the author to attempt to bring an alleged conspirator in the Kennedy assassination to justice. Inspired Oliver Stone to make the film *JFK* with Kevin Costner playing Garrison.

Robert J. Groden, *The Killing of a President: The Complete Photographic Record of the JFK Assassination, the Conspiracy and the Cover-Up*. New York: Viking Studio, 1993. A comprehensive visual record of the Kennedy assassination, alleged conspiracy, and following cover-up with 650 photographs, maps, drawings, and documents pertaining to the crime. Author was the first person to seriously analyze the Zapruder film and was a consultant on Oliver Stone's *JFK*.

Tom Hayden, *Reunion: A Memoir*. New York: Random House, 1988. Autobiography by a man whose disillusionment after the Kennedy assassination propelled him to found the anti–Vietnam War organization Students for a Democratic Society (SDS).

Mark Lane, *Plausible Denial*. New York: Thunder's Mouth, 1991. A book that alleges that the CIA was tied to the assassination of John F. Kennedy.

Mark Lane, *Rush to Judgment*. New York: Thunder's Mouth, 1992. The first dissection of the Warren Report—and the number one best-seller of 1966. Author calls into question nearly every aspect of the commission's findings from Oswald's background to the single-bullet theory.

David S. Lifton, *Best Evidence*. New York: Macmillan, 1980. A comprehensive examination of Kennedy's autopsy and X-ray photos that concludes the president's body was tampered with in order to remove evidence of a second gunman.

Harrison Edward Livingstone, *Killing Kennedy and the Hoax of the Century*. New York: Carroll & Graf, 1995. Develops the theory that the famous Zapruder film showing Kennedy being shot is a fake that has been used to cover up what really happened.

Harrison Edward Livingstone and Robert J. Groden, *High Treason*. New York:

Carroll & Graf, 1998. Puts forth the proposition that Kennedy was murdered by a secret team of government operatives who wanted to push the United States into the Vietnam War against the president's objections. First published in 1980 by the author of three other books concerning the assassination.

Jim Marrs, *Crossfire: The Plot That Killed Kennedy*. New York: Carroll & Graf, 1989. The diverse theories and facts about the Kennedy assassination, and one of the main sources used by Oliver Stone for *JFK*.

John Newman, *Oswald and the CIA*. New York: Carroll & Graf, 1995. A comprehensive and well-researched exploration of ties between the Central Intelligence Agency and the alleged assassins of JFK based on tens of thousands of formerly classified government documents.

Gerald Posner, *Case Closed: Lee Harvey Oswald and the Assassination of JFK*. New York: Random House, 1993. One of the few books concerning the Kennedy assassination that supports the findings of the Warren Commission and attempts to disprove well-known, but unproven, findings of conspiracy researchers.

Report of the Warren Commission on the Assassination of President Kennedy. New York: McGraw-Hill, 1964. Summary of the twenty-six volumes of material generated by the official investigation into the president's death by a panel headed by Supreme Court justice Earl Warren.

Anthony Summers, *Conspiracy*. New York: Paragon House, 1989. A definitive book on the Kennedy assassination with evidence alleging that the CIA and Mafia teamed up to kill the president.

Noel Twyman, *Bloody Treason*. Rancho Santa Fe, CA: Laurel, 1977. Examines the theory that a cabal of right-wing extremists, military officers, gangsters, and corrupt government officials plotted the assassination of JFK.

Charles G. Wilber, *Medicolegal Investigation of the President John F. Kennedy Murder*. Springfield, IL: Charles C. Thomas, 1978. A study by a leading forensic coroner of the medical procedures surrounding the Kennedy autopsy.

Internet Sources

Salvador Astucia, "Chapter Six: Other Garrison Findings," *Opium Lords*, April 2002. www.jfkmontreal.com/other_garrison.htm. A comprehensive site that pulls together many conspiracy theories surrounding the JFK assassination.

Mae Brussell, "The Last Words of Lee Harvey Oswald." http://www.ratical.org/ratville/JFK/LHO.html, May 28, 1992. A site by a well-known conspiracy researcher with various quotes by Oswald during the last days of his life.

Ronald L. Ecker, "Hell in Miami," *Hodge & Braddock*, May 17, 2002. www.hobrad.com/acrehell.htm. May 17, 2002. A site that alleges that various Mafia bosses were involved in the Kennedy assassination.

Mark Edwards, "Dirty Politics—Nixon, Watergate, and the JFK Assassination," *Tripod*, 1999–2000. http://mtracy9.tripod.com/kennedy.html. A thoroughly researched site linking former president Nixon to Kennedy's murder.

Edward Jay Epstein, "Question of the Week," Question of the Day. http://edwardjayepstein.com/question_oswald2.htm. A site with information about Oswald's attempted assassination of Major General Edwin Walker.

Craig Frizzell and Magen Knuth, "Did President Kennedy Plan on Splintering the CIA?" JFK and the CIA: Mortal Enemies? http://mcadams.posc.mu.edu/jfk_cia.htm. A site that questions whether Kennedy was going to take power away from the CIA after the Bay of Pigs fiasco.

"Governor Connally's Wrist Wound and CE-399," Warren Commission Exhibit CE-399—The Magic Bullet. www.jfk-info.com/fragment.htm. A site that examines the testimony before the Warren Commission concerning the single bullet that allegedly caused seven wounds in Kennedy and Connally.

House Select Committee on Assassinations, "The HSCA on Jack Ruby's Mafia Links." http://ourworld-top.cs.com/mikegriffith1/id153.htm. Excerpts from the HSCA report that link Ruby and Carlos Marcello.

"Introduction," The Corsican Connection. http://members.optushome.com.au/tnorth/introduction.htm. A site based on the findings of Stephen Rivele that ties Corsican Mafia hit men to the Kennedy assassination.

JFK Lancer Online Resources, "HSAC Report excerpt on Col. Jones." www.jfklancer.com/RobertJones.html. A site

with statements from various people who testified before the congressional committee formed in the mid-seventies to investigate the Kennedy murder.

Nicholas Katzenbach, "The Big Lie Begins," JFKLancer, 1996–2001. www.jfklancer.com/Katzenbach.html. A memo from the deputy attorney general to President Johnson, published by a Kennedy assassination conspiracy website.

Kennedy Assassination Home Page, "Findings of the Select Committee on Assassinations in the Assassination of President John F. Kennedy in Dallas, Tex., November 22, 1963," http://jfkassassination.net/russ/jfkinfo/hscareport.htm. A site containing the 256-page overview concerning the findings of the House Select Committee on Assassinations which investigated the murder of JFK in the mid-1970s.

George Lardner Jr., "Archive Photos Not of JFK's Brain, Concludes Aide to Review Board Staff Member," Washington Post, November 10, 1998. www.jax-inter.net/~cheryl/news.html. An article from the Washington Post concludes that the photographs of Kennedy's brain stored in the National Archives are of a brain other than the president's.

"The Lincoln/Kennedy Coincidences." http://www.generate74.com/pockett/presidents.html. A page with facts shared by the assassinations of Abraham Lincoln and John F. Kennedy.

Lee Harvey Oswald, Ed Butler, and Carlos Bringuier, "FPCC [Fair Play for Cuba] Debate over Station WDSU," Kennedy Assassination Home Page. http://jfkassassination.net/russ/jfkinfo3/exhibits/st

uck3.htm. A rare glimpse into the life of Lee Harvey Oswald from a radio debate recorded several months before the assassination in which Oswald talks about his political beliefs and his life in the Soviet Union.

Ashley Overbeck, "Prominent CIA-Press Relationships," *The CIA and the Media*, 1996. www.parascope.com/articles/0997/ciamedia.htm. A series of articles based on factual information about how the CIA recruited reporters, editors, and publishers of major American media institutions during the 1950s, 1960s, and 1970s.

Dave Reitzes, "Oswald and Ruby," LHO and Ruby. www.acorn.net/jfkplace/03/JA/DR/.dr06.html. A site that explores allegations that Oswald and Jack Ruby were acquaintances.

Oliver Stone and Zachary Sklar, "JFK (1991)," *FilmWritten Magazine*, 1999–2000. www.filmwritten.org/reviews/1991/jfk.htm. A site that reviews Stone's *JFK* with various quotes from the film.

Noel Twyman, "The French Connection," *Doug's JFK Assassination Page*. http://www.geocities.com/metsman_2001/french.html. A site that deals with the alleged Mafia conspiracy to kill the president.

Dr. Cyril Wecht, Testimony Before the House Select Committee on Assassinations, 1978. www.jmasland.com/testimony/hsca_med/wecht.htm. Medical expert testifies about Kennedy autopsy.

Index

Picture Credits

About the Author

Stuart A. Kallen is the author of more than 150 nonfiction books for children and young adults. He has written on topics ranging from the theory of relativity to the history of rock and roll. In addition, Mr. Kallen has written award-winning children's videos and television scripts. In his spare time, Stuart A. Kallen is a singer/songwriter/guitarist in San Diego, California.